RANGA CHAND'S

GETTING STARTED WITH MUTUAL FUNDS

RANGA CHAND'S

GETTING STARTED WITH MUTUAL FUNDS

**Ranga Chand *with*
Sylvia D. Carmichael**

Published in 1996 by
Stoddart Publishing Co. Limited
34 Lesmill Road
Toronto, Canada
M3B 2T6
Tel. (416) 445-3333
Fax (416) 445-5967

Stoddart Books are available for bulk purchase for sales promotions,
premiums, fundraising, and seminars. For details, contact the
Special Sales Department at the above address.

Canadian Cataloguing in Publication Data

Chand, Ranga
Ranga Chand's getting started with mutual funds

Includes index.
ISBN 0-7737-5757-0

1. Mutual funds.   I. Carmichael, Sylvia.   II. Title.
III. Title: Getting started with mutual funds.

HG4530.C52 1995   332.63'27   C95-931157-2

Cover design: the boy 100 & Tannice Goddard
Text design: Tannice Goddard
Author photograph: Peter Paterson

Printed and bound in Canada

*Stoddart Publishing gratefully acknowledges the support of
the Canada Council and the Ontario Arts Council in the
development of writing and publishing in Canada.*

To Jason

Contents

Acknowledgements

We would like to express our thanks to Jack Stoddart, Nelson Doucet, Donald G. Bastian, and Angel Guerra of Stoddart Publishing for their advice, enthusiasm, and unfailing support. We are especially grateful to Kevin Linder, our editor at Stoddart, for extremely helpful editorial advice. As always, he was there when we needed him and contributed enormously to the style, organization, and content of the manuscript.

A special thank you to our son Jason for his patience and continued computer assistance and to Hamish for ensuring that we got our daily walk.

Introduction

Although mutual funds have been around since the 1920s, it was not until the declining interest rates of the 1990s happened that sales really took off. Fuelled by this growing demand, mutual fund companies searched the world seeking new investment opportunities. Mutual funds had become — in Hollywood jargon — a "hot property," with everyone rushing to get a piece of the action. Mutual fund companies in Canada now manage over 170 billion investment dollars. It should come as no surprise that these same companies spend millions of dollars advertising their funds to ensure their market share of your investment dollars. Along with their glossy fund brochures, most of these companies also include equally glossy information kits aimed at educating potential customers about the ins and outs of investing in mutual funds.

Yet with all this information readily available, many Canadians still don't fully understand what mutual funds are, how they work, or which ones — if any — they should invest in. This puts investors in a very vulnerable position. Do you invest in something you don't understand? Do you rely on the advice of a professional? Do you throw up your hands in frustration and stay with GICs and Canada Savings Bonds? Whatever you decide, nagging doubts often remain.

There is no doubt that mutual funds can offer big investment opportunities for small amounts of money

— in some cases as little as $25 a month. In order to take full advantage of these opportunities, however, you must know enough to ask the right questions and understand the answers. While there are many books available on investing in mutual funds, most of those books assume a certain level of expertise on the part of the reader. The aim of *Ranga Chand's Getting Started with Mutual Funds* is to make investors and would-be investors aware of the basics and give them the knowledge and confidence to invest successfully in mutual funds. So let's take a look at mutual funds together and find some simple answers to all the important questions. But, before we start, let's get one thing straight: you don't have to spend hours every week poring over the business section of the newspaper, or have a flair for mathematics to understand and invest successfully in mutual funds. All you need is some common sense and a little time and effort. Remember, no one has a deeper interest in your financial future than you.

1

THE BASICS

1

Why Invest in Mutual Funds?

In the past, many of us relied on savings accounts, Guaranteed Investment Certificates, and Canada Savings Bonds in order to put something aside for a home, our children's education, our retirement, or that proverbial rainy day. Although we were at the mercy of prevailing interest rates, "investing" was too complicated, too time-consuming, or something only the wealthy could afford.

Today, people's attitudes have changed. Massive restructuring in the economy, with its inevitable job losses and wage freezes, and uncertainties over our financial future, including lingering doubts about the continued availability of government and company pension plans, have made us all look more closely at how we can get the best return on our money. This search has led us, rightly or wrongly, in unprecedented numbers to mutual funds. Rightly, because many mutual funds do offer excellent opportunities to help us achieve our financial goals. Wrongly, because many people have unrealistic expectations or unknowingly invest in poor performers. But for investors who take the time to do a little homework, mutual funds offer the following key benefits.

Diversification
This simply means holding a wide variety of investments. In other words, don't put all your eggs in one basket.

Let's assume you have $1,000 to invest. The most you can hope to purchase as an individual investor is a small number of stocks. By holding a stock, you own a share in a corporation's earnings and assets — anything the corporation owns. Even if the company performs well and your shares increase in value, your transaction costs — the money you pay your broker to buy and sell the stocks — will eat into, or maybe even wipe out, any profit you might make. If the company does badly and your shares decrease in value, you will lose money.

If, however, you put that same amount of money in a mutual fund that invests in stocks, you get diversification by the truckload. Your mutual fund may hold stocks in anywhere from fifty to over a hundred companies and in many different industries such as automobiles, pharmaceuticals, and banking. Now, if one of the fund's stocks does badly, the others may still do well. Spreading your money in this way among many different companies and industries effectively reduces your risk — the possibility that you may lose money. This diversification is one of the biggest advantages of mutual funds.

For most of us, the amount of disposable income and investment knowledge required to accomplish similar diversification would be mind-boggling. Also, sharing expenses with millions of like-minded investors, through a mutual fund, significantly reduces your investment cost. Because a mutual fund combines the assets it holds in trust for you and other investors, it is known as an "institutional trader" and as such can buy securities at wholesale prices. Bulk shopping, investment style! That's not something you and I could ever do, but certainly something we can benefit from.

Professional Management

Mutual funds are run by either an individual manager or a team of professionals who generally bring relevant academic qualifications and years of experience in analysing data, choosing securities to meet the fund's objectives, and deciding when to trade the holdings. That would be an overwhelming task if you were to attempt it on your own. By investing in a well-managed mutual fund, you share the expense of hiring someone with a proven track record. Your $1,000 will receive the same careful attention, and get the same returns, as the money of the institutional investors, such as pension funds, who place billions of dollars a year. It is extremely important to keep in mind, however, that fund managers, like hockey coaches, are not all equal. Some are much better than others.

Performance

For many people, the attraction of mutual funds is the possibility of higher returns on their investment dollar. This is especially true during periods of low interest rates. Investors should not assume, however, that all mutual funds will provide these higher returns. While many do, some don't. Of the 1,200 mutual funds currently available, over 130 have consistently delivered above-average returns in their respective categories (see *Ranga Chand's World of Mutual Funds* for details). A clear indication that many funds do achieve their investment objectives.

Too many funds, however, fall far short of attaining their stated goals. There are an astonishing 149 mutual funds that have consistently posted below-average returns over the past one-, three-, and five-year periods, and some funds, believe it or not, have underperformed for over ten years.

Although past performance is no guarantee of how a fund will perform in the future, it is doubtful whether any investor would *knowingly* put his or her money into a fund that has consistently underperformed compared to similar funds. Chapter 18 (Doing Your Homework) shows you how to avoid these underperformers and zero in on above-average funds.

Ease of Investment

Buying a mutual fund is not complicated and can be done in person, by telephone, or by mail. Most mutual fund groups also offer toll-free telephone assistance if you need additional information or help in filling out the forms. You may prefer speaking with someone in person and having them complete the necessary paperwork. Who you finally sit down with will depend on the funds you have selected. This could be the mutual fund salesperson at your bank or trust company, your broker or financial planner, or in some cases your insurance representative. We'll discuss more about who sells what in Chapter 2.

Liquidity

Mutual funds are extremely liquid. This means that it is easy to get at your money if you need it. It is not as quick as withdrawing money from your bank account, however. Units can be redeemed (sold back to the fund) at any time, and your money will generally be available by the next business day or, at the latest, within five business days. Some real-estate funds may take longer. To redeem any or all of your units in a mutual fund, you merely fill in the necessary forms provided by the company. If you need any help, simply call the company's toll-free number. Some companies may require a letter of redemption with your signature verified by your bank or trust company. After the mutual fund company receives the authorization, your money will be either sent to you in the form of a cheque or deposited directly into your bank account. Some companies also allow redemption by telephone or fax, provided you authorize this when you initially buy units in the fund.

Flexible Investing

The usual minimum initial investment for a mutual fund is $500, with subsequent investments starting at $25. Some mutual fund companies, however, now allow initial investments as low as $25 provided you invest on a regular basis through a pre-authorized investment plan. This means you agree to invest $25 or more at specified periods during the year. For example, you can decide on $25 every two weeks or $100 every month. The amount and the frequency depend on the options offered by the company. Once you have decided, this money will be automatically withdrawn from your chequing account on the specified dates. For those on a limited budget or with poor savings habits, this is a good way to start building towards future financial objectives. By investing the minimum $25 a month over a thirty-year period and given an average annual rate of return of 10%, you can accumulate nearly $57,000. If, however, you increase your savings period to forty-five years, that amount grows to roughly $265,000. That's over a quarter of a million dollars from a total investment of $13,500. Not bad for a non-saver on a limited budget!

Record Keeping

Along with investing, unfortunately, comes the task of maintaining records. This is where mutual funds can take a load off your shoulders. All mutual fund companies provide unitholders with regular statements detailing all transactions, income earned, and the total value of all funds held. Moreover, when you buy or sell units in a mutual fund, you automatically receive written confirmation. If, however, you expect to receive a cross between a share certificate and a Canada Savings Bond certificate when you buy units in a mutual fund, you are going to be disappointed. The only notification you will receive is a very ordinary looking typewritten confirmation detailing the number of units involved, the price, and the date of the transaction. Some fund companies do issue share certificates as evidence of ownership for a small fee.

Unitholders also receive yearly statements detailing the tax status of all earnings from the fund, including dividends and capital-gains information. The fund company issues either a T3 or a T5 slip for tax purposes, listing the type and amount of income you must report on your income-tax return. It is important to keep these papers in a safe place — perhaps in a large envelope or file for each fund you own units in. Of course, if your mutual funds are sheltered in a registered savings plan (RSP), you don't have to worry about paying taxes until you withdraw your money. You will also receive periodic reports giving information about the status of the fund, its investments, and any proposed changes. All you have to do is spend a few minutes reading the material. (See Chapter 20 for tips on how to stay on top.)

Key Points to Remember

- Mutual funds provide quick access to your money.
- Twenty-five dollars is all you need to start.
- Mutual funds offer uncomplicated diversification.
- Mutual funds make investing easy and simplify record keeping.
- Mutual funds give small-dollar investors big-dollar purchasing power.

2

What Are Mutual Funds?

A mutual fund is quite simply a collection of stocks, bonds, or other securities owned by a group of investors and managed by a professional investment company. When you put money into a mutual fund, it is combined with money from similar-minded investors. This large pool of money gives you much greater purchasing power than you could possibly have investing on your own. "Pooling" of money is neither complicated nor exclusive to the mutual fund industry. If, for example, you and your co-workers put your money together to buy lottery tickets, you already know how "pooled" money works. On your own, you might be able to afford one or two tickets, but your money combined with your co-workers' gives you a share in a great many more.

Most experts agree that as an individual investor, you would need anywhere from $50,000 to $100,000 to create a suitably diversified portfolio. For the average Canadian, that's a lot of money. That is why millions of investors now own units in mutual funds. According to the Investment Funds Institute of Canada, assets under management have shot up nearly fifteenfold, climbing from about $10 billion in 1985 to more than $146 billion in 1995. During this period, the number of shareholder accounts also increased sharply, rising from less than one million to more than fifteen million. Approximately one in four households, or seven million Canadians, now own at least one mutual fund.

Mutual funds are popular because they make investing in financial markets easy. Funds invest your and other unitholders' dollars in equity and debt securities. An equity security is a stock or share in a corporation's earnings and assets such as land, buildings, or machinery. Debt securities include bonds and money-market instruments. A bond is an IOU issued by a government or corporation certifying how much you have loaned it and the terms of the loan. Money-market instruments are short-term (less than one year) debt securities such as treasury bills, certificates of deposit, or commercial paper. The investment objectives of the fund determine which of these securities the manager buys. If the objective is "maximum growth" then the manager invests in equity securities, as traditionally the stock market has provided the highest returns. This type of fund, not surprisingly, is known as an equity mutual fund.

Who Sells Mutual Funds?

Unfortunately, when it comes to purchasing mutual funds, there is no such thing as one-stop shopping. Who you buy your mutual funds from will, to a large extent, depend on whether you choose a load or a no-load fund.

Load funds — mutual funds that charge a sales commission either at the time of purchase or when you sell back units — are generally not sold directly to the public by the mutual fund companies. Instead, these companies rely on independent sales representatives such as brokers, discount brokers, and some financial planners to promote their products; hence the sales commission. Some insurance and individual mutual fund companies, however, sell their funds through their own salespeople.

No-load mutual funds — funds that charge no sales commissions — are generally offered by banks, trust companies, and some individual mutual fund companies. These mutual funds are sold directly to the public. Don't jump to the conclusion, however, that you can walk into any one of these institutions and buy *any* no-load fund. Each financial institution and mutual fund company sells only its own funds. In other words, the Royal Bank will offer investors Royal Bank funds. It does not sell any other mutual fund company's funds. Similarly, Phillips Hager & North, a Vancouver-based mutual fund company, sells only its own funds. The Toronto Dominion Bank, however, recently announced plans to offer third-party funds, starting with the funds of about half a dozen well-known mutual fund companies.

Brokers offer the widest selection of mutual funds to choose from — in some cases up to 400 or 500 funds. Since brokers are not salaried employees, however, but rely on the sales commissions from the financial products they sell in order to make a living, the majority of these will be load funds. Moreover, many brokers and financial planners promote only a short list of funds, from five or six mutual fund companies.

How Does a Mutual Fund Make Money?

Mutual funds make money by investing unitholders' money in stocks, bonds, and other securities that earn dividends or interest, and by selling these investments at a higher price than originally paid. The money (such as interest income from bonds) earned from a fund's investments is paid to unitholders as *income distributions*, while any profits from selling these investments at an increased price are paid out as *capital gains distributions*. Unitholders can also make a capital gain or capital loss when selling back their units to a fund, depending on whether the unit price has increased or decreased since the units were purchased. Funds also pass on to unitholders responsibility for the annual income tax payable on such distributions.

The mutual fund company makes its money through the management fees charged to unitholders. Although all the glossy brochures telling you which fund to buy and why are free, investing in a mutual fund is not. This is discussed in more detail in Chapter 3, "How Much Will It Cost?"

How a Fund Works

Managing a fund obviously requires some degree of skill, combined with long hours, the necessary support staff, and the crucially important computers and software. On a day-to-day basis, a fund manager or team of professionals must review the previous day's market performance, compare their fund's return with others, and analyse the economic news and indicators that are affecting the value of the fund. They must also buy and sell securities, such as stocks or bonds, that meet the objectives of their specific fund, and research possible new markets.

On the administrative side, there are, among many other activities, new accounts to be opened, cheques to be mailed, questions to be answered from new and existing clients, and detailed accounts to be kept of each and every buy and sell transaction. All this bookkeeping is usually completed by the end of each business day, when the new net asset value (NAV) of the fund must be reported. Most funds report their NAV daily, although some may report weekly or monthly. This figure is quoted the next day in the business section of many newspapers, under mutual funds. Look under the column headed NAV per share.

What Is the Net Asset Value?

The net asset value of a mutual fund is the dollar value of one unit of the fund and is calculated by dividing the current market value of the fund's assets, less liabilities, by the number of units already sold. For example, if the fund you are interested in has assets worth $200 million, after deducting liabilities, and there are 10 million units already sold, each unit is worth $20 ($200 million divided by 10 million). This means you would pay $20 for one unit of the fund. If you bought 100 units, you would pay $2,000. In this example, no matter how many people buy or sell units in the fund, the NAV will remain unchanged at $20.

The only way the NAV will change is due to the rise or fall in the market value of the assets held by the fund.

Let's say that the same fund's assets increased to $300 million due to some great investment decisions of the fund manager and the number of units outstanding (sold) remained unchanged at 10 million. The net asset value of each unit you held would now be worth $30 ($300 million divided by 10 million). Anyone now buying into the fund would have to pay the new NAV of $30 per unit. If you decided to sell, you would have made a capital gain of $1,000, the positive difference between the price you originally paid ($2,000) and the price you received when you sold ($3,000). On the other hand, if you decided to stay with the fund, this capital gain would be paid out in the form of a distribution, usually by being reinvested in additional units. The NAV would then fall by the amount of the per-share distribution.

Of course, if the markets took a tumble or the manager made some poor investment decisions, the reverse would be true. The NAV would drop, and if you decided to sell at that point, you would suffer a capital loss.

The NAVs of most mutual funds will fluctuate, some more than others; you should be aware of this before purchasing. The NAV for some equity funds, for example, may be up one month and down considerably the next. You won't panic and make a bad investment decision if you know what to expect.

Safety

Mutual funds are not the same as savings deposits, Guaranteed Investment Certificates, or Canada Savings Bonds. There is no guarantee that the money you invest in a mutual fund will remain intact, or even grow. As mutual funds are "securities," not "deposits," they are not insured by the Canada Deposit Insurance Corporation (CDIC). Whether you purchase mutual fund units at your local bank, trust company, or broker, *they are still not insured*. All assets in a mutual fund, however, are kept separate from the mutual fund company and are held in trust by a Canadian chartered bank or trust company, and as such are protected under banking and trust laws. This segregation is important. It means that even if the company itself collapses, the assets of the mutual fund are protected. These safeguards do not mean that the value of your investment will not increase and decrease in value. Mutual funds are not a magic carpet ride to continuous high returns. Many funds have decidedly bumpy rides, some even nosedive. The extent to which your investment fluctuates will, of course, depend on the type of fund you hold and the expertise of the manager.

The bottom line here is that although mutual funds are not insured, there are many safeguards in place to ensure that no one runs off with your money. There is no guarantee, though, that the $1,000 or $10,000 you invest in a mutual fund will remain intact, or even grow.

Key Points to Remember

- The NAV is the price of one unit in a mutual fund.
- NAVs fluctuate — some more than others.
- Mutual funds are not insured.
- Load funds charge sales commissions.

3

How Much Will It Cost?

Before you buy units in any mutual fund, it is important that you know exactly how much it is going to cost. All charges are, of course, listed in the simplified prospectus. That is one good reason to read this document very carefully. (A prospectus is the selling document legally required to be distributed to mutual fund investors. Chapter 19 highlights the important points.) If you are still not sure of the fees involved, don't panic. Either telephone or visit your mutual fund sales representative and get him or her to explain the fee structure. If this means the salesperson has to take extra time to go over the various fees involved, so be it. If you would feel more comfortable with a written, itemized list of all the fees pertaining to your choice of fund, based on the amount of money you are investing, ask for one. For example, if you are investing $5,000, what will be the exact dollar amount of your fees on an annual basis? Above all, don't feel pressured into signing on the dotted line. Take your time, go home, think it over. You should do this in any case.

Management Fees

All mutual funds charge a management fee. It doesn't matter if you buy from a bank, trust company, broker, or the mutual fund company's own salesforce, you will pay a management fee. It doesn't matter if it is a load or a no-load fund, you will still pay a management fee. These fees are usually given as a percentage of the fund's total assets and pay the administrative costs and the wages and bonuses of fund managers. Funds charge anywhere from less than 0.5% for some money-market funds to nearly 4% for certain international funds. Management fees are deducted before the quoted performance numbers are calculated. This means that if you are interested in a fund with an 11.4% annual rate of return, this fee has already been deducted. In other words, you won't get billed personally. It comes off the top. That's why many mutual fund unitholders are completely unaware that their fund charges this fee.

To give you some idea of the amount of money we are talking about, let's assume you bought units in a fund with total assets of $2 billion and a management fee of 2%. The management fee for that particular fund would be $40 million annually. Make no mistake, we are talking big money here. This is where mutual fund companies make their profits. Moreover, this amount is paid whether the fund performs well or not. You may have to postpone your trip to Florida because of poor returns but the fund manager won't! Management fees are non-negotiable. There is no bargaining. If they say 2%, that's exactly what they mean.

Management fees for load funds (funds that charge a fee at the time of either purchase or redemption) may vary according to which option you choose. For instance, in one company, the management fee is 2% if you opt for a front-end load, 2.25% for a back-end load, and 2.5% for their no-load option. Get the salesperson to calculate how much your original investment would be worth, assuming (say) a 10% annual rate of return, over different time frames such as five, ten, fifteen, or even twenty years, using the different options. You will then be in a position to make a more knowledgeable decision.

Management Expense Ratio

For a more accurate measure of the up-front cost to the investor, check out the management expense ratio

(MER). It sounds highly mathematical but it is quite simply the total of all other expenses charged to the fund, plus the management fee, expressed as a percentage of the fund's total assets. For example, if a fund with $1 billion of assets has total yearly expenses of $20 million, its MER is 2% ($20 million divided by $1 billion). This means that out of every $100 you have invested, $2 goes to management expenses.

To ensure that they get their market share of your investment dollars, many mutual fund companies also provide independent salespeople (like brokers) with promotional incentives such as all-expenses-paid trips to annual sales conferences in locales like San Diego, Las Vegas, and Florida. These incentives increase the MER and decrease returns to unitholders. Moreover, there could be an inherent conflict of interest for the sales representatives, as pointed out in the recent Ontario Securities Commission's report, "Regulatory Strategies for the Mid-'90s — Recommendations for Regulating Investment Funds in Canada," prepared by Glorianne Stromberg. Acting on the recommendations contained in the Stromberg Report, the Investment Funds Institute of Canada (IFIC) has submitted a draft code of sales practices as the basis for "voluntary" compliance by institute members. The draft code recommends that these promotional incentives be prohibited. IFIC is the lobbying and educative association of the Canadian investment funds industry. Its membership is made up of mutual fund management companies, retail distributors (such as brokers and financial planners), and members of the legal, accounting, and other professions.

Trailer Fees

A trailer fee is the annual service commission paid by the mutual fund company to your sales representative. This fee is paid as long as you hold units in the fund. These fees generally range between 0.25% and 1% and are paid out of the fund's management expenses. There are two points you should consider here. First, a trailer fee is a *service* commission. This means your salesperson should be providing you with ongoing services such as answering questions about your account, tax information, the performance of your fund(s), and other related matters. As pointed out, however, in the Stromberg Report, "no one monitors whether in fact the services have been provided," and "these fees may also be a factor in a sales representative not recommending a change in the client's portfolio when it would be in the client's interests to make such change." The Stromberg Report has recommended that the mutual fund industry voluntarily end the payment of these fees.

Second, through the practice of graduated trailer fees — commissions that may, for example, start at 0.25% but end up at 1% as the amount of clients' money builds up — some sales representatives could be receiving tens of thousands of dollars each year. The IFIC Draft Code has recommended that these graduated trailer fee payments be prohibited, thus removing the incentive for sales representatives to funnel clients' money into a particular fund. It does not, however, ban trailer fees in their entirety as recommended in the Stromberg Report. This means that some fund companies might pay a flat rate of 0.25% while others might pay 0.5% or even 1%. Therefore, the inherent conflict of interest still exists. Is the sales representative recommending a particular fund because it is the best fund for you or because it pays a high trailer fee? Not all mutual fund companies pay trailer fees to sales representatives.

Front-End Load

A front-end load is a sales charge paid by you at the time of purchase to your mutual fund salesperson. This sales commission can be as high as 9%, although most companies recommend a maximum of 5% or 6%. The amount is negotiable with your mutual fund representative. When you see the words "maximum" or "up to" next to fees, it means you can bargain. This sales charge is deducted from the amount you invest. If you have $5,000 to invest and, due to your great bargaining skills, end up paying a front-end load of 3%, the actual amount of money invested is $4,850 ($5,000 minus $150). If you cannot get the salesperson to negotiate the fee, shop around. The betting is you can find someone else who will — especially if mutual fund sales are low.

Back-End Load

A back-end load is the fee charged to investors when they redeem, or sell back, their units to the fund. This fee is usually staggered, with earlier redemptions paying a higher fee — a policy designed to discourage early withdrawals. A typical range starts at 5% or 6% for redemptions during the first two years and decreases to 0% after seven to ten years. The redemption fee schedule given below is typical of many funds.

During the 1st year	6.0%
During the 2nd year	5.5%
During the 3rd year	5.0%
During the 4th year	4.5%
During the 5th year	4.0%
During the 6th year	3.0%
During the 7th year	2.0%
Thereafter	Nil

Suppose you opt for the back-end load. Unlike with the front-end load option, this way your entire $5,000 goes to work for you immediately. There is no deduction when you purchase. If, however, you decide to sell back your units after three years, you have to pay the 5% redemption fee at that time.

Let's say your fund has made some modest gains and your original investment of $5,000 is now worth $6,000. Some funds base the redemption fee on the original amount invested. In this case, if you decide to redeem after three years, you must pay $250 (5% of $5,000). So you receive $5,750 ($6,000 minus $250). Other funds base the charge on the market value of your units at the time of redemption. This means you pay $300 (5% of $6,000) and take home only $5,700. Obviously, in this case, the first way is a better deal. If, on the other hand, your investment has declined in value, the reverse is true.

Choosing the back-end load allows all of your investment dollars to go to work for you immediately. But because most back-end loads are usually fixed (some companies might negotiate), you should be committed for the longer term to avoid paying these fees.

Before purchasing a load fund with the back-end load option, you should also be aware that although you don't pay a fee directly to your sales representative at the time of purchase, the mutual fund company does. This, of course, increases its costs. As a result, you may be paying a higher MER. Over the longer term, this higher MER could eat into your returns more than a one-time front-end load. Another point to keep in mind is that if the fund does not perform as well as expected, due to a change in management or other circumstances, or if there are better opportunities elsewhere, you may be reluctant to switch because of the high penalty.

No-Load Option

Some load companies offer a no-sales-commission option. Again, check the MER. It will probably be higher than either the front-end or back-end load MERs. Over the longer term, this could significantly decrease your returns.

Redemption Fees

Some funds charge an early-redemption fee if you sell back your units within ninety days of the initial purchase. This charge can range from a flat fee of $100 to up to 2% of the initial value of your holdings. This means if you have invested $9,000, you can end up paying a fee of $180. Other funds, although they quote a redemption fee in their prospectus, waive this charge. Again, call and ask and get it in writing before you buy.

Distribution Fees

These fees may apply if you buy a load fund and choose the back-end load option. Distribution fees are paid annually from your account to your salesperson, either by a deduction from any distributions or by redemption of some of your units. Distribution fees (usually between 0.25% and 0.5% or in dollar terms between $2.50 and $5.00 out of every $1,000 invested) are calculated on the net asset value of your holdings. These fees typically increase along with the value of your investment for a predetermined period (normally seven to nine years). Some funds, however, charge this fee for as long as you hold units in them! In other words, if you invest $10,000, and the distribution fee is the lower rate of 0.25%, you start with payments of $25 a year. If your $10,000 increases to $15,000, you will pay $37.50 annually. It might not seem like much in the beginning, but over the life of your investment these costs can mount up to several hundred dollars and significantly reduce the overall return on your investment.

Other Costs

Switching Fees. Most banks and trust companies, and some mutual fund companies, allow you to transfer from one fund to another within their family of funds — for example, from XYZ's bond fund to XYZ's equity fund — at no cost or for a small fee of around $10. Do not assume, however, that your chosen fund falls into this category. A few companies charge anywhere from 2% to a maximum of 9% of the amount being switched. This means if you transfer $8,000 from one fund to another, you can end up paying anywhere from $160 to $720. If you are switching because the fund is a poor performer, this additional cost will only make matters worse. You should also keep in mind that switching — selling units in one fund and buying units in another — may have tax implications if your investments are held outside of an RRSP.

Set-up and Closing Fees. Some companies charge a nominal fee (around $50) to open or close an account.

Handling Fees. If you purchase no-load funds through an independent source such as a broker, you may be charged a handling fee of around $50 on amounts under $100,000 and $100 for amounts over $100,000. Because you are purchasing a no-load fund, the salesperson should not charge you a sales commission. The handling charge compensates them for the time they spend with you filling in the necessary forms.

RRSP/RRIF Fees. An annual administration fee (between $25 and $75) and termination fee (typically around $15) may be charged. Also, switching fees of up to 2% of your holdings may apply with some funds. This may not seem like much, but if you have $60,000 and you want to re-invest in another fund, it can cost you up to $1,200. Keep this in mind if you are aggressively investing for your retirement. Moreover, if you are in the fortunate position of having $200,000 — which is not unrealistic towards the end of any retirement savings plan — a 2% switching fee will cost you $4,000. Not the kind of money you want to part with if it can be avoided.

If there is anything you do not fully understand about a fund's fees, call or visit your fund company's nearest office. This will also give you a good opportunity to get an idea of the type of service and attitude of the company. If you are not satisfied with the answers you receive or with the level of service, you may want to reconsider buying that particular fund. If you are buying from an independent sales representative, you also need to know if he or she is being paid a trailer fee. If so, make sure you receive ongoing service.

A Final Word

The IFIC Draft Code has recommended that clear and complete disclosure of all compensation payable to distributors be provided in summary form on the inside front cover of a mutual fund's prospectus. Investors should be aware that the recommendations contained in the IFIC Draft Code are, for the moment, just that, and IFIC does not have the power to enforce them.

Key Points to Remember

- All mutual funds charge a management fee.
- Check out the management expense ratio.
- Get the dollar value of your annual fees.
- Sales commissions and high trailer fees may influence a sales representative's recommendations.
- Ask questions and shop around.

4

The Different Types of Mutual Funds

A t first glance, mutual funds seem to present a dizzy-
ing array of products geared to just about every possible investment need. It is enough to make anyone but
the most committed investor run back to the more familiar territory of GICs and Canada Savings Bonds. But
don't get overwhelmed. Although there are over 1,200
mutual funds to choose from and no two are exactly
alike, they fall into several broad-based categories.

Money-market and treasury-bill funds are the most
conservative mutual funds and invest primarily in
government (or equally safe) securities. These funds
generally pay two or three percentage points higher rates
of return than savings accounts and are extremely safe.

Fixed income funds invest in some combination of treasury bills, debentures, bonds, and mortgages. The aim of
fixed income funds is to provide high, regular income
payments with the possibility of some capital gains.

Equity funds invest in common and preferred shares of
Canadian companies and are recommended for investors seeking long-term growth through capital gains. An
investment time frame of at least five years is generally
recommended for this type of fund.

Balanced funds provide a combination of income and growth by investing in a mixed portfolio of common stock, preferred shares, bonds, and cash. This type of fund is suitable for investors with limited dollars or who want a more diversified portfolio in one fund.

Special equity funds invest in areas such as real estate, resources, and precious metals. Due to the specialized nature of these funds, returns tend to be dramatic, both positive and negative. The experienced investor will have, at most, only a small percentage of his or her portfolio invested in these funds.

Dividend funds invest in dividend-paying preferred shares of Canadian corporations and in common shares that are expected to yield a high level of dividend income. As with equity funds, there is the potential for long-term capital growth. Dividend funds also receive preferential tax treatment.

Global and international funds invest in money-market securities and in bond and stock markets in various countries and regions of the world. These funds offer investors the opportunity to increase returns through extra diversification. If Canadian markets are doing badly, China, Japan, or Europe may nevertheless be doing well.

This survey of fund categories should give you a good idea of the range of investment possibilities. For a more detailed look at any of these categories, turn to the relevant chapter in Part 2.

Before you invest in any fund, however, there are two important factors to consider: a fund's investment objectives and its level of risk. Both of these should be given equal weight when making an investment decision. Failure to do so could prove hazardous not only to your finances but also to your mental well-being.

A Fund's Investment Objectives

Every mutual fund has a specific investment objective, and it is the job of the fund manager to buy and sell securities to attain that goal. In general, these objectives are safety of capital, income, and growth. A fund that seeks to provide safety of capital as its main objective will look for ways to protect your initial investment from loss. Income funds, on the other hand, will aim to provide investors with stable and regular payments in the form of a monthly or quarterly cheque. Funds that aim for growth will invest in equity securities to increase the value of the fund's assets and provide investors with long-term capital gains. Some funds seek to provide a combination of income and growth, and sometimes all three objectives, in one package.

As an investor, you have to decide which investment objectives match your own and concentrate on those particular funds. Mutual funds never invest at random, and neither should you. The more clearly you define your investment objectives, the easier it will be to identify appropriate mutual funds. More about this in Chapter 15.

A Fund's Level of Risk

To find the funds that are best for you, you have to understand the concept of investment risk. Risk is, simply put, the possibility that an investment may go down in value or not perform as well as expected. No investment, whether domestic or international, is risk free. That's a fact you should not ignore. Even money lying securely in a savings account is at risk from inflation. Some common risk factors are:

Credit risk. The possibility that the company holding your money will not pay the interest or dividend due, or the principal amount when it matures.

Inflation risk. The risk that the dollar you get when you sell will buy less than the dollar you originally invested.

Interest-rate risk. The possibility that a fixed debt instrument, such as a bond, will decline in value due to a rise in interest rates. Chapter 9 tells you why.

Market risk. The risk that the unit price or value of your investment will decrease.

One fundamental rule applies to all investments. The smaller the risk, the smaller your potential return. The higher the risk, the higher the potential reward. How much risk you should take depends to a large extent on your investment objectives. The further away from your financial goals or the younger you are, the more risk you can afford to take. This is because the ups and downs of financial markets tend to even out over time. Remember, historically the stock market has risen steadily regardless of its temporary declines. The closer to your financial goals or the older you are, the less time you will have to make up any losses.

You should also examine your own feelings with regard to risk. Are you the type to rush off and buy units in an overseas equity fund with the expectation of receiving high returns year after year? If you are, stop for a moment to consider how you would feel if the fund posted a -20% return. Would you panic and sell? If you had fully understood the level of risk associated with buying the fund, you might well have been prepared to ride out its volatile yearly returns.

Taking an ultra-conservative approach to investments, however, is also subject to risk. By investing in only the "safe and familiar" such as GICs and Canada Savings Bonds, you run the risk of shortchanging yourself over the long term. While a 7% guaranteed rate of return may look attractive today, inflation or increased taxes could reduce it to a real rate of return of only 2% or 3% further down the road. All investors would like the high returns without the risk. To achieve higher returns, however, you must be willing to live with some risk and be prepared to stay put.

Most financial experts stress that in order to minimize

risk, you should hold a well-balanced investment portfolio. If you put $4,000 into a single investment, such as one company's stock, you give yourself very little cushion should it falter. Let's say that the stock market declines by 10%. You will suffer a capital loss of $400. If you had put $2,000 into a bond fund and $2,000 into an equity fund, your capital loss would be reduced to $200. On top of that, bond markets may have performed well, decreasing your loss further.

To a large extent, by investing through mutual funds, we relieve ourselves of the time-consuming and almost impossible task of researching each investment opportunity and its possible risk. Instead, we rely on the knowledge and expertise of a fund manager, or a team of professionals, to buy and sell the best investments at the right time. Some mutual funds have excellent track records. Some do not. Doing your homework before you invest will reduce the risk of investing in the latter. Chapter 18 shows you how.

What Is Volatility?

There is a lot of talk about a fund's volatility. But what exactly is it, and, more importantly, should you be worried about it? Volatility is a measure of the historical variability in a fund's rate of return compared with similar funds. In other words, when you take into account the returns on all mutual funds, some funds will have wider swings in returns than others. Factors that can contribute to a fund's volatility include the type of assets held, degree of diversification, sector, country or region of investment, use of derivatives, turnover and quality of portfolio holdings, and management investment style. For example, a fund that invests in Government of Canada treasury bills, which are perceived to have no credit risk, is less volatile than one that invests in shares of small new companies. Similarly, a fund that invests in many countries, because of its diversification, is going to be less volatile than a fund that invests in only one country.

One widely accepted measure of risk is standard deviation. Standard deviation is a statistical measure of the (say) month-to-month ups and downs of a fund's return relative to the average, or mean, monthly return for the fund over the period. In this way, standard deviation allows us to compare funds with similar investment objectives over a particular time frame. It can also be used as an indication of how much more risk a fund in one category has than a fund in another category. To arrive at a volatility rating, we compare a fund's standard deviation with all other funds' standard deviations and classify it into one of ten deciles. A low volatility rating of 1 indicates a fund with a stable monthly rate of return. The higher the volatility rating, the wider the swings in rate of return.

Beta value is another statistical measure of volatility, which tells you how much a fund or security moves in relation to the market. For example, the TSE Total Return Index (TRI) has a beta value of 1. A fund with a beta value of 1.05 would move up or down about 5% more than the TRI. The higher the beta, the greater the volatility.

The following chart shows the average volatility rating, and the volatility range from the lowest to the highest, for each mutual fund category. Since a minimum of thirty-six months of data is needed to compute standard deviation reliably, funds that have been in existence for less than three years do not have a volatility rating.

| TYPE OF FUND | VOLATILITY RATING | |
	Average	Range
Canadian		
Money-Market	1.0	none
Short-Term Bond & Mortgage	1.6	1–2
Bond	2.5	2–3
Dividend	2.5	2–4
Balanced	2.6	2–4
Equity	3.5	2–8
Small-to-Mid-Cap Equity	4.6	3–10
Special Equity	5.0	1–9

TYPE OF FUND	VOLATILITY RATING	
	Average	Range
International		
Money-Market	1.2	1–2
Bond	2.3	2–3
Balanced	2.8	2–4
U.S. Equity	3.5	2–5
International Equity	3.7	3–5
European Equity	4.3	4–5
Emerging Markets	5.5	5–6
Asian Equity	6.2	4–8

Source: *Ranga Chand's World of Mutual Funds*

As you can see, all Canadian money-market funds have a volatility rating of 1. This means the volatility of these funds will not be a factor in deciding which money-market fund to invest in. When you look at Canadian equity funds, however, although the average volatility rating for this group is 3.5, the range goes all the way from a low volatility rating of 2 to a high of 8. If you invest in this type of fund, its volatility rating should most certainly influence your choice.

The following chart shows the returns over the past ten calendar years of various mutual funds with different volatility ratings. Of course, every fund is different, but the chart will give you some idea of what to expect.

TYPE OF FUND	85	86	87	88
Cdn. Money-Market	9.7	8.8	8.0	8.9
Canadian Equity	20.6	1.3	-6.6	12.5
Asian Equity	35.2	*61.5*	26.8	4.1
Special Equity	16.3	14.2	1.2	14.0

89	90	91	92	93	94	VOLATILITY RATING
11.6	*12.5*	9.0	6.0	4.4	*4.2*	1
24.1	-6.5	16.5	10.2	*30.9*	3.3	4
6.3	*-27.1*	7.1	-5.9	35.3	21.1	7
-3.8	*-27.8*	-10.0	31.9	*85.3*	-13.4	9

As you can see, the spread between the highest return and the lowest return (both italicized) is much less for a fund with a low volatility rating of 1, compared with a fund with a volatility rating of 7 or 9. Although over time these wide fluctuations in returns get smoothed out, the roller-coaster ride may be too much for some investors to take. For example, the value of your investments will not always move in an upward direction. Returns will vary from one period to another, sometimes showing a significant decline. This could mean the value of your investment drops from $10,000 to $8,000. If you are unaware of or uncomfortable with this volatility, it could lead to selling at the wrong time at considerable loss.

Your goal, therefore, should not necessarily be to invest in the fund with the highest returns regardless of its volatility. Your goal should be to invest in a fund with a good track record that meets your investment objectives and has a level of volatility that you can comfortably live with. Keep in mind that two funds can *average* the same return but perform very differently. One fund may earn 11% one year and 13% the second. The other fund may earn 25.4% the first year but have a return of 0% the second. Through the law of compounding, both funds average 12% a year. Everything else being equal, most investors would prefer the steady performer.

If, on the other hand, you are comfortable investing in a fund with a high volatility rating, you should expect to earn more than the market in good years and lose more in bad years. The key is to stay with a fund long enough so that your gains will substantially outweigh your losses, in order to justify the risk. Regardless of your comfort level, however, you should ask the sales representative to provide you with a fund's annual returns over, if possible, the last five or ten years. This will give you a very good idea of its volatility. That way, if you decide to invest, you do so with your eyes wide open.

You can easily compare the volatility ratings of all mutual funds in their specific categories by looking at the monthly mutual fund surveys in the *Globe and*

Mail and *Financial Post*. Look under the "Volatility" or "Standard Deviation" heading. The average for the group is given at either the beginning or the end of each fund category.

As a final word, keep in mind that there are many investment options that are less secure than mutual funds. The single-issue aspect of investing in a bond, stock, real estate, or antiques may make these investments more vulnerable than even some of the riskier equity mutual funds.

Key Points to Remember

- Funds fall into several broad-based categories.
- Mutual funds never invest at random.
- Match a fund's investment objectives to your own.
- Risk is the potential for losing money.
- No investment is risk free.
- The higher the risk, the higher the potential return.

5

Management Styles

Many people investing in a mutual fund take little or no account of the investment style of the fund manager. But a particular manager's investment style is not something that should be ignored. Investors are well advised to look at a manager's investment philosophy as well as a fund's past performance figures before making a buying decision. Fund managers usually adhere to one of the following approaches.

Growth

These managers look for companies with a good track record of rapid growth in sales and earnings and the potential for more of the same. Typically, a growth stock will have a higher-than-average price-to-earnings ratio and trade at a price well above book value. The belief is that the future growth of the company will, in a relatively short time frame, justify its stock's current high price and provide even higher prices in the future. Growth investments will often be in the small-to-medium-capitalization companies.

Value

Managers who follow a value approach search for assets that are undervalued or where the manager feels the market may not be appreciating the full potential for that company or industry. Typically, these stocks sell at low price-to-earnings ratios or book value, or may have hidden assets such as real-estate or trademark rights. The strategy is to buy the assets cheap and sell them when their market value rises.

Sector

These managers focus on specific industries such as high technology or chemicals that, based on their analysis, will experience the greatest growth. The investment portfolio will then be built around individual companies within these selected industries. Some sector investors attempt to forecast which areas of a market will do well in the short term. Their strategy is to get in at the bottom before other investors catch on.

Many managers use a blend investment style, employing a combination of value, growth, and sector strategies.

Top-Down

Managers who use a top-down approach first analyse the economy and market outlooks and then select markets and industries that they feel will outperform. These managers are more concerned with the big picture rather than individual companies.

Bottom-Up

Fund managers who follow a bottom-up management style start by selecting promising individual companies, with little or no emphasis on the larger picture. Only stocks or bonds that meet these managers' investment criteria are purchased. If they can't find what they want, they will hold cash until they do.

Some fund managers combine top-down and bottom-up styles by determining not only the countries and industries in which to invest but also the individual companies.

Interest-Rate Anticipation

When actively employed, this technique covers forecasting and analysing the direction of the change in interest rates, the degree of the change across maturities, and the timing of the change. Any anticipated drop in interest rates would dictate an increase in the duration of the bond portfolio, and the opposite action would be called for when rates are expected to rise. The greater the shift of the duration prior to the change in rates, provided the manager's forecast and timing are correct, the greater the incremental returns.

Spread Trading

This approach involves switching bond issues to take advantage of higher yields or to decrease risk without adversely affecting the yield. Spread traders analyse and closely monitor credit risk, historical yield relationships, and the yield curve. Unlike interest-rate anticipators, spread traders are very active market participants.

Although many managers remain true to their investment philosophy, others use a combination of two or more styles. None of these investment styles is better or worse, only different. Read the prospectus and annual report or call the fund company if you have any questions on a particular manager's style.

6

Mutual Fund Returns

A return is a measurement of how much an investment has increased or decreased in value over any given time period. In particular, an annual return is the percentage by which it increased or decreased over any twelve-month period. Suppose you invest $1,000 today and twelve months later your investment is worth $1,070. The annual return on your original investment of $1,000 is 7%, or $70. The real return, however — the annual return less the rate of inflation over the investment period — will be lower.

Calculating a Fund's Total Return

For those with a mathematical bent, figuring out the return on a mutual fund is not difficult. For the rest of us, a calculator comes in handy. Suppose the XYZ Fund has a net asset value (NAV) of $10 at the beginning of 1995. During the year, distributions of $2 per unit are made to investors. At the end of the year, the NAV is $13.50. To figure out the fund's total return, you start with the year-end NAV of $13.50 and add on the distribution of $2.00. This gives you a total of $15.50. Next, subtract the original NAV of $10.00. That leaves you with $5.50, the fund's profit for the year. Finally, divide the $5.50 by the starting NAV of $10.00, which gives you 0.55. To arrive at a percentage, simply multiply by 100. The total return for the XYZ Fund for 1995 was 55%.

$$\frac{\text{Final NAV} + \text{Distributions} - \text{Original NAV}}{\text{Original NAV}} \quad \text{X } 100$$

$$= \frac{\$13.50 + \$2.00 - \$10.00}{\$10.00} \quad \text{X } 100$$

$$= \frac{\$5.50}{\$10.00} \quad \text{X } 100 \qquad = 0.55 \text{ X } 100 = 55\%$$

How to Calculate Your Return

Let's say you have invested $1,000 in a mutual fund and reinvested all distributions of $200. (If you received any distributions in cash, remember to include them.) At year's end, your account is worth $1,200. To calculate your return, first subtract your initial investment of $1,000. Then take the difference of $200 and divide by your initial investment of $1,000. Multiply the answer, 0.2, by 100 to arrive at 20%.

$$\frac{\text{Current value of units} - \text{Initial investment}}{\text{Initial investment}} \quad \text{X } 100$$

$$= \frac{\$1,200 - \$1,000}{\$1,000} \quad \text{X } 100 \quad = \quad \frac{\$200}{\$1,000} \quad \text{X } 100$$

$$= 0.2 \text{ X } 100 = 20\%$$

These calculations can be used for any twelve-month period, or any other period.

When calculating your own return, keep in mind that any sales commissions or transaction costs (see Chapter 3) have to be deducted from the current value of your units and will therefore reduce your return.

Compound Average Annual Returns

Compounding means that on top of earning a return on your original investment, you also earn returns on your returns. The compound average annual return quoted in mutual fund brochures and advertisements shows the total a fund has returned, taking into account all capital gains (or losses) and dividends, expressed as an average yearly growth percentage.

For example, in its advertising, a certain fund quotes a three-year compound average annual return of 7.6%.

This does not necessarily mean the fund delivered this figure in any one of those three years. In fact, this particular fund delivered -8.8% for the year ending December 31, 1994, +21.6% for the year before, and +12.4% for 1992. Only if you had invested at the beginning of 1992, and reinvested all distributions, would your compound average annual return for the three years have been 7.6%. If you had invested at any other time, your rate of return might have been higher or lower.

The compound average annual return is an important measurement, as it shows the rate at which wealth grows over time. This is something that you, as an investor, clearly need to know.

A Final Word

Returns on any fund will reflect the particular market it invests in. For example, you cannot realistically expect an equity fund to deliver a return of 25% if the stock market is down 10%. Moreover, even if a fund shows a positive return, you might not; it may take you some time to recoup any transaction costs.

Key Points to Remember

- Returns show how your investment has increased or decreased in value.
- Compounding earns returns on your returns.
- Compound average annual returns show how wealth grows over time.
- Transaction costs reduce returns.

7

Taxes and Mutual Funds

E ven if you are strictly an RRSP investor, you should read this section. It will give you some idea of what taxes you could be paying if your funds were not in a tax shelter. It may also give you additional incentive to put as much as possible into your RRSP while you can (who knows when the federal government will revise the rules?). Of course, having your money in an RRSP doesn't let you off the tax hook for ever. They get you when you eventually withdraw your funds.

After deducting expenses, mutual fund companies pass on all income to unitholders annually. This means unitholders must pay the taxes due on all income earned on mutual funds held outside of an RRSP. This includes all interest, dividends, and capital gains. The fund company pays taxes on the management fees charged, loads, and any other fees they receive as income. Any investment income you receive is subject to tax at your marginal tax rate (the tax rate payable on the last dollar you earn), although dividends and capital gains receive preferential treatment.

Interest income received from mutual funds is subject to tax at your marginal rate and receives no preferential tax treatment. This means that if your marginal tax bracket is 43%, you will pay taxes of $43 for every $100 of interest income you receive.

Dividend income. Although Canadian corporations have already paid taxes on their earnings before paying dividends to your mutual fund, you must still declare these dividends for tax purposes. By claiming the dividend tax credit, however, you will reduce the amount of tax payable. This is accomplished by first grossing up your dividend by 25%, then multiplying the result by 13.33%. Let's assume you receive $2,000 in dividend income:

$2,000 x 125%   = $2,500.00
$2,500 x 13.33%   = $333.25

Your dividend tax credit in this case would be $333.25, and that would be the amount claimed when calculating your federal tax payable.

Capital gains can be made either by selling units in a fund, and getting back more money than you originally paid, or by receiving a capital gains distribution from the fund itself. The amount subject to tax can be reduced by adding any charges, such as a front-end load, to your purchase price and subtracting any expenses incurred, such as redemption fees, from the sale price before calculating the amount of tax owed. A capital loss — when you sell units in a mutual fund for less than you paid — can also be used to reduce any capital gains. Otherwise, 75% of your capital gains are added to your base income and taxed accordingly. This means that out of every $1,000 in capital gains earned, you get to keep $250 tax free. The remaining $750 will be taxed at your marginal tax rate.

The actual amount of tax paid by an individual will vary, of course, depending on the type of income earned, his or her base income, and the province they live in.

Common Tax Errors

Many investors have the mistaken notion that by reinvesting distributions they avoid paying tax. Whether you reinvest all distributions or receive a cheque in the mail, you will still have to pay tax on them. Also, while switching from one fund to another within a group of funds has become quite commonplace, many investors don't realize the tax implications. When you move money between funds, you are selling units in one fund and buying units in another. Revenue Canada will expect you to pay taxes on any gains. Moreover, if it is near the end of the year and you are thinking of buying units of a fund, it is important to ask when the next distribution will take place. Suppose you buy units on December 12 and the fund makes a distribution at year's end. You are responsible for paying taxes on the distribution, even though you have been a unitholder in the fund for less than a month.

Finally, for tax purposes, it is especially important to keep accurate records. To do this, keep all fund company statements and written confirmations of each transaction in a safe place.

Key Points to Remember
- Interest income receives no special treatment.
- Reinvested distributions are subject to tax.
- Check distribution dates before investing.
- Keep all mutual fund statements in a safe place.

8

Registered Retirement
Savings Plans

Are you concerned about the long-term effects of high government deficits? Worried that government and company pensions will be unable to provide an adequate income in your retirement years? If you answered no, I sincerely hope it's because you are independently wealthy. If you answered yes, welcome to the club. It means you are aware of the potential financial problems that could derail your retirement plans and lifestyle. It probably also means that you are already contributing to a Registered Retirement Savings Plan (RRSP). If you aren't, you should be.

What Is an RRSP?

A Registered Retirement Savings Plan is a tax shelter provided under the Income Tax Act (Canada) to give individuals the incentive to save towards their retirement. By investing carefully and wisely, many Canadians enjoy a comfortable standard of living in their later years. An RRSP in itself, however, does not automatically guarantee this. It merely provides the vehicle.

By contributing to an RRSP, you increase your savings in two ways:

All RRSP contributions are deductible for tax purposes, subject to certain limits. For 1995, the contribution limit is 18% of your previous year's earned income, less any pension adjustment, or the allowed maximum of $14,500 — whichever is the lesser amount. The limit for 1996 and 1997 is reduced to $13,500. Whatever your eligible 1995 contribution, be it $5,000 or $14,500, this money can be deducted from your total earned income for the year, reducing the amount of tax you pay — and, more importantly, increasing the amount of money you keep. When you make your RRSP contribution, you will receive a tax receipt, which should be filed with your tax return in order to claim your deduction. Beginning in 1991, if you did not contribute your maximum amount in any one year, you can carry forward the unused portion to subsequent years. Make sure you do not exceed the $2,000 lifetime overcontribution limit. Any amount in excess of this limit carries a penalty of 1% a month until the amount overcontributed is withdrawn. Confirmation of your RRSP contribution limit appears on your previous year's Revenue Canada Notice of Assessment.

Any income earned is not taxed. This means that all monies contributed to and accumulating in an RRSP, including all capital gains and interest income earned, is left untouched by Revenue Canada until withdrawn. All RRSPs must be terminated by the end of the calendar year in which your seventy-first birthday falls. This means that if you turn seventy-one years of age in April, you have until the end of December of that same year to terminate your plan. At termination, the money accumulated in your RRSP can be either transferred to a Registered Retirement Income Fund (RRIF), used to purchase an annuity, or cashed in. You can also choose a combination of these options. The difference between an RRSP and a RRIF is quite simple. RRSPs are set up to accumulate money, whereas a RRIF's function is to pay out money — with minimum amounts set each year. An annuity typically provides fixed monthly payments for as long as you live. If you decide to cash in your plan, the trustee (bank or trust company) will withhold tax at source before releasing the funds. This amounts to 10% for withdrawals up to $5,000, 20% for amounts up to $15,000, and 30% for higher amounts. By contrast, if you transfer all monies accumulated in your RRSP to a RRIF and withdraw on a monthly basis what you need, subject to the required minimum amount, then only those amounts over the minimum annual payouts will have tax withheld at source.

Why Contribute to an RRSP?

Trying to save even the smallest of nest eggs outside a registered plan is, for most of us, increasingly difficult. The combined effects of taxation and inflation can eat into returns in a surprisingly rapid manner. Assume that you invest $1,000 of pre-tax income at the beginning of each year for thirty-five years, and that your annual rate of return is 8%. At a marginal tax rate of 45%, you are left with only $550 to invest annually. At the end of thirty-five years, you will have accumulated $46,000. By contrast, the same $1,000 invested in an RRSP will have built savings of $186,000. A difference of $140,000. Even if you withdraw the entire $186,000 from your RRSP at the end of the thirty-fifth year, without taking advantage of any further tax-deferral plans such as a RRIF, you will have $102,000 after tax. That still puts you ahead $56,000.

When to Start

Probably the last thing someone just starting out in the workforce wants to consider is retirement. After all, you are young, and you finally have some money in your pocket and many plans on how to spend it. Retirement is something you intend to worry about later on down the road.

Unfortunately, the further down the road you travel before acting, the more it will cost you. Let's say that at age thirty, you contribute $1,000 — that's less than $90 a month — at the beginning of each year for thirty-five years, and achieve a very realistic 8% rate of return. By age sixty-five, even if you do absolutely nothing else, you will have accumulated close to $190,000. If, however, you wait until further down the road, say age forty-five, and contribute for only twenty years, you will have less than $50,000 in your plan. A difference of nearly $140,000. Moreover, the longer you wait, the greater the difference.

When to Contribute

Your current year's RRSP contribution must be made on or before March 1 of the following year. Many people, however, wait until the last possible moment — so much so that February is known as the "RRSP season." But by delaying your contribution until this late date, you effectively miss out on fourteen months' income. Another option is to make regular contributions through a pre-authorized investment plan. These plans are offered by most financial institutions and major fund companies. All you have to do is decide how much and how often, and your contributions will be automatically deducted from your bank account and invested into the mutual fund of your choice. Whether or not you choose a pre-authorized investment plan, don't forget to name a beneficiary when you open your RRSP, to avoid probate fees.

If you have fallen into the bad habit of putting off making your contribution until the last possible moment, you should strive to correct this. Try to contribute as early as possible, each and every year. It could make a significant difference to your retirement income.

Retirement Goals

You should define all investment goals, including retirement. Fuzzy thinking is not the way to go. Here are some questions to get you started. Turn to Chapter 15 for more on investment objectives.

- When would you like to retire? In five years or twenty?
- Where will you live? Mortgage-free home or rental?
- How much annual income will you need? More or less than your current income?

- What sources of income can you expect? Government or company pension plan?

Most banks, trust companies, brokers, and financial planners have information kits or can personally help you plan your RRSP portfolio. Many financial institutions also offer free RRSP seminars, investment workshops, or videos. Take advantage of any additional help you can get. By taking the time now, you can enjoy the benefits later.

Spousal RRSPs

You may invest all or a portion of your own maximum allowable RRSP contribution to a plan in your husband's or wife's name. Assume your allowable contribution is $12,500. If you decide to contribute $7,000 to your own plan, then you will be able to contribute the difference of $5,500 to a spousal RRSP. This contribution is deductible from your taxable income, but the plan belongs to your spouse and the amount contributed by you will not affect his or her yearly limit. Because a spousal RRSP belongs to the person in whose name the plan is registered, only that individual can make any withdrawals or changes to the investments held in the plan.

Although only the planholder can withdraw funds from a spousal RRSP, the withdrawals will be taxed in one of the following two ways. These rules cease to apply, however, if you and your spouse are living separately at the time of withdrawal.
- Any amounts withdrawn will be taxed in the planholder's name, provided the contributing spouse has not made any contributions in the year of withdrawal or the two preceding years.
- If the contributing spouse has made contributions during the year of withdrawal or the two preceding years, the amount withdrawn, up to the amount of such contributions, will be included in the contributing spouse's income.

The advantages of a spousal RRSP are more significant when one partner earns a significantly higher current income (or is the sole wage earner) and expects to receive a higher retirement income. Contributions to a spousal RRSP can mean two lower tax brackets at retirement instead of one higher one. Provided you have earned income, you can still contribute to a spousal RRSP until your husband or wife reaches age seventy-one — even if you yourself are over seventy-one.

Self-Directed RRSPs

This kind of plan gives you much broader investment options, including a more diversified choice of mutual funds, term certificates from a wide range of issuers, Canadian and foreign stocks and bonds, or even your own mortgage. This wide range of investment alternatives makes a self-directed RRSP attractive to many investors. You do not have to be an investment guru to manage this type of plan. As you accumulate your funds within a regular RRSP, however, your aim should also be to accumulate investment knowledge. This will put you in a favourable position to consolidate your RRSPs into a single self-directed plan at a later stage.

One of the benefits of this kind of plan is that you can contribute investments you already hold. If you find yourself short of cash one year, you can instead contribute any Canada Savings Bonds or stocks that you hold. A self-directed plan also allows for easier record keeping, and transferring to an annuity or RRIF will be simpler.

The Foreign-Content Limit

Although the foreign-content allowance for an RRSP is 20%, many financial planners advise allocating only about 15% or 17% of the book value (the original price you paid) of your total holdings. This gives you a cushion for future gains without exceeding the limits set by Revenue Canada. Wealthier and more aggressive investors can also boost their international content by investing in Canadian-based mutual funds that invest up to 20% of their funds in international securities. In this way, the total foreign-content limit can be increased to a maximum of 36%.

Let's suppose you have $10,000 to invest. You can purchase $2,000 worth of international funds on your 20% foreign-content limit. But if you invest the remaining 80%, or $8,000, in Canadian mutual funds that also take advantage of the 20% foreign-content limit, you boost your total foreign holdings by another $1,600 (20% of $8,000). This gives you a total foreign content of 36%, or $3,600.

Most financial institutions and brokers will monitor the foreign-content portion of your RRSP. The bottom line, however, is that it is your responsibility, and if you do go over the limits set, you will end up paying a 1% monthly tax penalty on any amount over the 20% foreign-content limit.

You may also find when you switch funds that the foreign-content limit has changed to reflect the current market value, not the price you originally paid. It is important to keep your original records of purchase in a safe place, in case you need to produce them later on for tax purposes.

Many financial experts recommend putting aside four to six months' living expenses as emergency money. In the real world, that's not always possible. If you have to withdraw any money for emergencies from your RRSP, try to keep it to a minimum. If you own units in different funds, seek advice as to which should be redeemed. Depending on the prevailing economic climate, redeeming units in, for example, a bond fund may make less of a negative impact than cashing in units in an equity fund.

A Final Word

Rushing out at the last minute and buying units in the first available mutual fund is definitely not the way to go. If your quality of life in retirement will depend to a large extent on how much you have accumulated within your RRSP, you should be prepared to do a little homework. If you end up with poorly performing funds in your RRSP, it could be a case of what you gain on the swings (tax deferrals), you lose on the roundabout (low returns).

Key Points to Remember

- Contribute as much as you can as early as you can.
- Any income earned in an RRSP is not taxed until withdrawn.
- Do not overlook spousal RRSPs.
- Self-directed RRSPs offer wider investment options.

2
THE FUNDS

9

Fixed Income Funds

The aim of any income fund, not surprisingly, is to provide investors with regular income payments while protecting capital. Of course, this type of fund is useful not only to people seeking additional income. Income funds are also a good choice for adding diversification to any investment portfolio. They invest mainly in, or in some combination of, bonds, debentures, and mortgages.

What Is a Bond?

A bond is a certificate of indebtedness recording the amount of the loan and the terms of repayment. The main difference between a bond and a debenture is that while a bond is secured by assets of the issuer, such as equipment or real estate (much like your mortgage is secured by your home), a debenture is backed only by the issuer's general creditworthiness. In other words, the issuer does not put up any specific assets to assure repayment of the loan.

Bonds are bought in either the primary or secondary markets. After a bond has been issued and sold to investors in the primary market, it can then be traded in the secondary market. The price you pay or receive will depend on current interest rates and other factors. Do not confuse these bonds with the familiar Canada Savings Bonds, which are not traded and are cashable at full face value plus any accrued interest at any bank at any time.

Bond jargon is like talking in another language. You don't have to be fluent, however — you only have to know the basics. Once you know the following key terms, you'll sound like a bond trader. More importantly, when it comes to buying a bond fund, you'll feel much better when you understand what the salesperson is saying.

Issuer. The body, such as a federal, provincial, or municipal government, public utility like Ontario Hydro, or corporation, that issues the bond. These government bodies and corporations need to borrow money to pay for such things as expansion of facilities, machinery, long-term capital work projects, or repayment of existing debt. In this way, they are not much different from the rest of us — except they need to borrow a lot more.

Issue date. The date on which the bond is issued and interest starts to accrue.

Term. The life span of the bond from the issue date to the maturity date. Short-term bonds mature in one to three years, medium-term bonds in three to ten years, and long-term bonds in anything over ten years.

Face value, par value, or denomination. The value that appears on the face of the bond certificate and is paid at maturity. If you purchase a $5,000 bond and pay the full face value, you have bought "at par." If, however, you pay $4,900 for that bond, you have bought "at a discount" (less than the face value), and if you pay $5,100, you have bought "at a premium" (more than the face value).

Maturity date. The date when the amount borrowed by the bond issuer must be paid back and interest payments stop.

Coupon. The fixed annual interest rate paid on a bond. Some bonds have coupons attached which you cut off on the due date and send in to receive your interest payment. Hence "coupon rate" instead of the more familiar "interest rate." If you buy a $10,000 bond at par maturing in five years with a 12% coupon rate, you will receive $1,200 in interest every year, regardless of whether current interest rates are higher or lower, until maturity.

Market value. The price you receive, for example, if you sell your bond before the maturity date. This could be higher or lower than the price you originally paid, depending on numerous factors such as current interest rates, the length to maturity of your bond, the financial health of the issuer, political uncertainties, and market rumours.

Yield. This describes the amount you actually earn from a bond, and is calculated by dividing the amount of money a bond will pay in interest by the price of the bond. Suppose you purchase a $5,000 bond at par (you pay the full face value) which has a coupon rate of 10%: you get $500 a year — a yield of 10%. If, however, you buy that same bond at a discount (less than the face value), say $4,500, you still get the $500 a year interest, but the yield has now increased to 11.1%. The larger the discount, the bigger the yield. But if you buy the bond at a premium (more than the face value), say $5,500, you still get the $500 a year interest, but now the yield is only 9.1%. The larger the premium, the lower the yield.

Yield to maturity. This is an even more accurate measure of a bond's true rate of return. It takes into account the interest rate in relation to the price, the purchase price versus the face value, and the number of years to maturity. Yield to maturity is not easy to calculate. Don't feel badly, however: even bond traders use computerized programs and special bond calculators to figure this one out.

Ideally, for you as an individual to invest successfully in the bond market, you should diversify by issuer and also by maturity. You do not want all your bonds to fall due on the same date, in case interest rates at that time are low. If you stagger the maturity dates by different years, you lessen this risk. Similarly, buying bonds of only one issuer is not without risk. What if a corporation, for example, loses a major contract or has senior management problems? The market value of your bonds might fall in value. As investing in bonds can cost anywhere from $5,000 to $50,000, the cost for this diversification is prohibitive and also requires considerable amounts of skill and time — which probably rules out most of us in one way or the other.

Bond Funds

These funds invest in short-, medium-, and long-term bonds and debentures of federal, provincial, and municipal governments and major corporations. Short-term bond funds are usually grouped with mortgage funds because of their similar maturity dates, generally one to five years, of the investments held. The aim of a bond fund is to provide investors with maximum interest income and capital gains from buying and selling bonds. For investors requiring additional income on a regular basis, bond funds generally pay more frequently than individual bonds. Unlike with an individual bond, however, when you invest in a bond mutual fund, there is no maturity date and no guaranteed repayment of the cash you invest.

The biggest advantage of bond funds is without doubt the diversification you can get with limited amounts of money. Your $1,000, instead of buying one bond, now buys you a share in many bonds from a wide variety of issuers with varying interest rates and different maturities. This minimizes your risk: if some bonds do badly, the others may do well. Unlike an individual bond, a bond fund gives no fixed rate of interest. The rate of interest paid by a bond fund fluctuates depending on the interest paid by the bonds held. The role of the fund manager is to capitalize on these changing interest rates. An experienced fund manager will anticipate a decline in interest rates and hold longer-term bonds at the higher rates. Conversely, if rising interest rates are anticipated, the fund may switch to securities with shorter maturities. When these fall due, the fund is then able to reinvest at the higher rates. A bond fund will realize either a capital gain or loss depending on the investment decisions of the fund manager.

How Interest Rates Affect Bond Funds

Bond funds, similar to individual bonds, are influenced by interest-rate movements. When interest rates go up, bond prices and the unit prices of bond mutual funds go down. Conversely, when interest rates go down, bond prices and the unit prices of bond mutual funds go up.

First, let's look at what happens when you buy a bond. Assume that today you buy a $1,000 bond at par (paying the full face value) with a coupon rate of 10%. The next day interest rates drop to 9%. If you decide to sell your bond, another investor may be willing to pay a premium (an amount more than the face value), perhaps $50, because your bond now offers a higher rate of return — 10% as opposed to 9%. If you sell, you receive $1,050, making a capital gain of $50. Of course, the opposite happens if interest rates rise, say to 11%. If you want to sell your 10% bond now, you have to offer it at a discount (an amount less than the face value). After all, if investors can now purchase a bond paying 11% interest for $1,000, they are not going to pay the same price for a bond paying only 10%. If you decide to sell, you may receive $950, realizing a capital loss of $50. If, however, you decide to hold your bond, you continue to collect interest at the coupon rate of 10% (regardless of whether current interest rates are higher or lower) and on maturity receive the full face value of $1,000.

Now let's look at a bond mutual fund. In this case, when interest rates go down, the unit price (NAV) rises. This means if you originally paid $1,000 for 100 units at a NAV of $10, these units may now be worth (say) $12 each. If you sell, you receive $1,200, making a capital gain of $200. If instead interest rates rise, your 100 units may now be worth only $9 each. If you sell, you receive

$900, realizing a capital loss of $100. If, however, you stay with the fund, your income payments may increase if the fund manager is in a position to reinvest maturing bonds at the higher rates of interest.

Bond Funds and Risk

When choosing a bond fund, you should be aware of the risks involved. *Credit risk* is the possibility that the issuer of the bond will not make the interest payments or repay the principal on maturity. Government of Canada securities are perceived to have virtually no risk, followed by provincial government bonds and high-quality corporate bonds. Issuers with the least credit risk generally offer lower interest rates than higher-risk issuers. *Market risk*, in the case of bond funds, is the risk that the value of your investment will decrease due to rising interest rates. Short-term bonds have the least market risk, followed by medium- and long-term bonds. An "AAA" rating, the highest, which is given by the Canadian Bond Rating Service and Dominion Bond Rating Service, indicates a fund with the highest degree of protection for principal and interest. This rating is followed by AA, A, BBB, BB, B, CCC, CC, and C in descending order.

Bond Fund Returns

The average return for Canadian medium- and long-term bond funds over the five-year period to December 31, 1995, was 10.6%, and returns ranged from a high of 13.8% to a low of 6.0% — a difference of 7.8%.

Income from bond funds is normally paid monthly or quarterly or can be reinvested in additional units. All Canadian bond funds are RRSP eligible.

Mortgage Funds

As with a bond fund, the aim of a mortgage fund is to provide regular income. This type of fund generally concentrates on residential first mortgages (the most secure type), guaranteed either by the Government of Canada or a Canadian bank, on prime residential properties located in major cities across Canada. It is therefore quite possible that you could invest in a fund holding your own mortgage. Most bank funds also guarantee to buy back any mortgages held by the fund, should they default. Some funds also include commercial and industrial mortgages in their portfolios.

Any changes in income payments made by this type of fund reflect the maturity dates of the mortgages held. As mortgages within a fund's portfolio mature, the fund manager has to reinvest in new mortgages, which may provide a higher or lower rate of interest depending on current interest rates. Because fund managers rarely trade the mortgages they hold, capital-gains potential is low. On the plus side, mortgage funds tend to be less volatile than most bond funds because of the shorter maturity dates — generally one to five years — of the investments held. The exception is mortgages on industrial or commercial property, which often have longer maturities.

Mortgage Fund Returns

The average return for Canadian mortgage funds and short-term bond funds over the five-year period to December 31, 1995, was 8.8%, and returns ranged from a high of 10.4% to a low of 6.8% — a difference of 3.6%.

Income from a mortgage fund is generated from the interest payments made on the mortgages held by the fund, and is usually paid monthly, quarterly, or semi-annually. All short-term bond and mortgage funds are RRSP eligible.

Key Points to Remember

- When interest rates go down, bond prices go up — and vice versa.
- Mortgage funds are less volatile than most bond funds.
- The shorter the maturity, the smaller the risk.
- Fixed income funds provide additional income and diversification.

10

Canadian Money-Market Funds

Money-market funds invest in short-term debt securities such as commercial paper, certificates of deposit, bankers' acceptances, and federal and provincial treasury bills (T-bills), all generically known as money-market instruments. This means the money you invest in a money-market fund is used for short-term loans to various Canadian companies and government bodies.

A money-market fund is the ideal place for money that will be needed in the near future, to keep an emergency cash fund, or to park your money while seeking more attractive investment opportunities. If interest rates are high, and the stock or bond market is looking unsettled, you may want to let the money sit until things calm down. These funds generally pay two or three percentage points higher rates of return than savings accounts and are extremely safe because of the short-term nature of the investments held. If safety of capital is your number one concern, you should choose a money-market fund that invests exclusively in treasury bills. This is as risk-free as you can get, because the Government of Canada stands behind the T-bills in the fund's portfolio. As money-market funds move away from Government of Canada treasury bills to provincial treasury bills and debentures issued by major corporations, the risk increases — but it is still extremely small.

The main difference between the assets held in money-market funds and bond funds is the term to maturity (the date on which the loan falls due). Some money-market securities mature in as little as twenty-four hours; others mature in ninety days or several months. The maximum maturity is 364 days. Keep in mind that the longer the maturity, the less quickly the fund manager will be able to exchange investments for ones with higher interest rates, should rates rise. If you think interest rates are headed up, you may want to put your money into a fund with shorter-term maturities. When the fund manager invests at the higher rates, the higher yields are passed on to you. Because money-market funds tend to turn over their portfolios very quickly, annual reports may not accurately reflect a fund's holdings. Call and ask for the maturity dates of its current holdings if you are in any doubt.

Unlike other mutual funds' unit prices, which reflect the market in which those funds invest, the unit prices of money-market funds do not fluctuate but are regulated to remain fixed at $10. This way, only the fund's yield fluctuates. When you are shopping for a money-market fund, you will notice that the advertisements usually give two rates of return — an indicated yield and an effective yield. The indicated yield is usually the amount actually earned by the fund during the latest seven-day period, annualized. The effective yield assumes that the fund will continue to yield this amount every week on an annual basis. That is, it assumes that the rate of interest will remain unchanged over the period of one year. This could be a rather large assumption. If, for example, interest rates decline, the effective yield could be considerably less.

One of the attractive features of this type of fund is that in most cases you can get your money out by the next business day. Some funds also offer chequing privileges with balances in excess of $5,000. Be sure to check the prospectus if you want cheque-writing privileges, because there can be restrictions on the minimum amount to be withdrawn and also on the number of cheques you can write.

Money-Market Fund Returns

Since the performance of money-market funds tends to cluster in a fairly narrow band (generally about 1.5% between the best and worst return), it makes little sense to buy units in funds that charge sales commissions. Clearly, the consistent performers that have the lowest management expense ratios and do not charge sales fees will have the edge. Load companies that offer a "family" of funds should be willing to waive this fee if you invest, or are already invested, in other family members. (Most mutual fund companies offer a family of funds which includes money-market, fixed income, and equity funds.)

Interest income from most money-market funds is paid by monthly cheque, deposited directly into your bank account, or is automatically reinvested in additional fund units. All Canadian money-market funds currently available are RRSP eligible.

A Final Word

About the only downside to investing in a money-market fund is that when interest rates are low, the interest the fund pays will also be low, and you could be earning more money elsewhere.

Key Points to Remember

- Money-market funds are a good short-term parking place.
- Money-market funds provide a couple of percentage points more than savings accounts.
- T-bill funds are the safest.
- The shorter the term of the securities held, the lower the risk.
- Buy a no-load.
- Zero in on management expenses for the best deal.

11

Canadian Equity Funds

These funds invest in a wide range of Canadian companies through common and preferred shares. The primary objective of Canadian equity funds is to provide capital gains for investors through increases in stock prices.

Stock Basics

A stock is a share in a corporation's assets such as buildings, land, machinery, and furniture, and a share in its profits if it does well. Corporations issue two types of stocks. Common stocks give stockholders voting rights and may also pay dividends. Holders of preferred stock, on the other hand, generally have no voting rights but must receive dividend payments before common stockholders.

Typically, a company goes public (issues stock for the first time) when it needs to raise money, usually for expansion. This is called an initial public offering (IPO). In exchange for this money, the management of the company gives up some of its control to the people who buy the shares. After the IPO, the shares are bought and sold on the stock market and the company makes no further money on these trades. Stock prices are set by supply (who wants to sell) and demand (who wants to buy) and are influenced by many factors such as economic trends, interest-rate movements, consumer confidence, political events in Canada and overseas, market rumours, and the financial health of the company.

Stocks in Canada are traded on a variety of exchanges including the Toronto Stock Exchange (TSE), which is by far the largest, followed by the Montreal Exchange (ME), the Vancouver Stock Exchange (VSE), the Alberta Stock Exchange, and the Winnipeg Stock Exchange. Foreign exchanges are located in major cities such as New York, London, Paris, Tokyo, and Hong Kong. Stock prices are listed daily in the business section of newspapers either by company name or an abbreviation such as RY for Royal Bank.

Bear markets — prolonged periods of falling prices in stocks — are usually brought on by the anticipation of a decline in economic activity. Bull markets — prolonged periods of rising prices — are characterized by high trading volumes. Bull markets usually occur over a longer period, while bear markets tend to happen quickly.

Why Invest in Equity Funds?

Historically, the stock market has provided the highest returns. That's one good reason for investing in equity funds. The second is the diversity you can get for much less money. Even if you have the know-how, with $1,000 or $2,000 you are not going to be able to buy a wide range of shares in various companies. By investing that same amount of money in an equity mutual fund that holds shares in many different companies, you get diversification by the truckload. This diversification greatly reduces risk. If one or two companies do badly, the others may continue to perform well.

Equity funds invest in a wide range of Canadian companies and their main objective is to provide capital gains for investors through price appreciation of the shares held. This means that when the fund manager buys shares in XYZ Company at $15 per share and later sells them at $25, the fund realizes a capital gain of $10 per share. All capital gains are passed on to unitholders in the fund in the form of distributions, normally at year's end. This can be paid to you by cheque, or you can elect to reinvest in additional units of the fund.

"Blue-chip" equity funds typically invest in large, well-established corporations, such as Imasco Limited, Bombardier Inc., and Power Corporation of Canada, with long histories of profitability and regular dividend payments. "Growth" funds may invest in shares of companies that have achieved above-average profitability in recent years and are expected to continue to do so. "Aggressive growth" funds, on the other hand, often invest in the common shares of small, emerging companies, often referred to as "small-cap," that are expected to grow rapidly. "Cap," or capitalization, is the total market value of a company and is determined by multiplying the current price of one share by the number of shares outstanding (sold). A company with 10 million shares trading at $10 each would have a $100-million market capitalization and would be considered a small company. Small new companies can often increase their sales very quickly because they are starting from such a small base. Their newness, however, can make them a riskier investment than well-established companies. Read the prospectus and annual report very carefully before you buy, to make sure the mutual fund is compatible not only with your investment objectives but also with your comfort level.

Buying units in an equity fund makes you a shareholder in the fund, not a shareholder in the corporations held by the fund. You have no voting rights in any of the companies the mutual fund holds shares in.

Investment Styles

There are various investment styles used by equity fund managers. *Growth* managers look for small- to medium-sized companies promising high revenue or earning increases and often pay high prices for companies they expect will show excellent potential. *Value* managers, by contrast, seek out stocks or securities that they feel are undervalued when compared to the company's actual earnings, cash flow, or book value. The reasoning behind this approach is the belief that sooner or later other investors will realize the true value of these companies and buy their stocks, thereby increasing the stock price. Some value managers will hold large stock or cash positions depending on the movement of the market.

Although many managers stick to one investment style, others show more flexibility depending on market conditions. The hallmark of a good fund manager is the ability to provide investors with consistently above-average returns. The hallmark of a good investor is the ability to identify and invest in those funds. For more on management styles, see Chapter 5.

Equity Funds and Volatility

The average volatility rating for Canadian equity funds is around 4 — 1 being low, 10 being high. (For more on volatility, refer to Chapter 4.) A few of these funds are very volatile, with a rating of 6 or more. One fund has a volatility rating of 10! If you are comfortable with this volatility, that's fine. If you are not, that's fine too. It does not mean you should not invest in equity funds. What it does mean is that, perhaps, you should select a less volatile fund, with a rating of 4 or below, or put only a small percentage of your investment dollars into the more aggressive fund.

Equity Fund Returns

Many people, discouraged by the returns on their GICs, have misconceptions and unrealistic expectations when it comes to equity funds. While it is true that, histori-cally, equity funds have provided a high average rate of return over the long term, this does not mean high rates of return year in and year out. Because of the volatility of the stock market, returns may be up dramatically one year but down considerably the next. You must be com-mitted to leaving your money in this type of fund for at least five years to take advantage of market peaks. In other words, you can lose money if you don't do your homework and pull out at the wrong time.

You should also bear in mind that not all equity funds provide investors with high rates of return. Some

Canadian equity funds, like some funds in other categories, consistently deliver below-average returns. It is therefore important to comparison shop before investing. Mutual fund salespeople, like car dealers, are not going to point you to a better deal at another dealership. They want to sell you their product, not someone else's! Also, as pointed out in Chapter 3 (How Much Will It Cost?), independent salespeople may be biased towards a particular fund company because of incentive considerations. The onus is on you to find the best deal. Chapter 18 tells you how.

The average return for equity funds over the five-year period to December 31, 1995, was 10.2%, and returns ranged from a high of 24.6% to a low of 2.7% — a difference of 21.9%. The average return for small-to-mid-cap equity funds over the same period was 16.0%, with returns ranging from a high of 32.9% to a low of 6.5%, for a difference of 26.4%.

A Final Word

The goal for all growth funds is capital appreciation, not regular income or price stability. This makes them an unwise choice for people who need extra cash on a regular basis or who may have to use the money for short-term goals or in an emergency. But investors who want to earn higher returns cannot afford to ignore equity funds.

Key Points to Remember

- Equity funds invest in stocks.
- A stock is a share in a corporation's assets.
- Stocks provide higher returns over the long term.
- All equity funds are risky as short-term investments.

12

Canadian Balanced Funds

As their name implies, Canadian balanced funds invest in a balanced portfolio of short-, medium-, and long-term bonds of federal and provincial governments and corporations and in stocks of Canadian corporations. The goal of this type of fund is to provide both growth and income in one investment. If you are a first-time investor in mutual funds or have only a small amount to invest, a balanced fund is a good starting place. Not only will it give you a well-diversified portfolio in one fund, but it will also provide you with an introduction to the various markets.

A typical balanced fund's asset mix might be 20% in money-market instruments, 40% in bonds, and 40% in stocks. These amounts will fluctuate depending on market conditions and the investment decisions of the fund manager. A fund's policy might also dictate the minimum and maximum amounts that can be invested in any one market. For example, a fund manager could have the option of placing 0%–20% in cash, 20%–60% in bonds, and 10%–60% in stocks. These ranges depend on the policies of each fund.

Balanced income funds place their investment emphasis on bonds for higher income potential, while *balanced growth* funds place greater emphasis on stocks for higher capital gains. If income is your primary investment goal, while still wanting exposure to the stock market, you should pick a balanced income fund rather than a balanced growth fund.

Asset allocation funds tend to get lumped together with balanced funds. However, the main difference — and it's a big one — between this type of fund and a balanced fund is that an asset allocation fund can invest up to 100% in stocks, in bonds, or in cash equivalents. If the fund manager believes the stock market is the place to be, then that's where most of the assets of the fund will be. The percentage, whether it be 80% or 93%, is entirely up to the fund manager; there is no fund policy on maximums and minimums to which the manager must adhere. The fund manager is free to hold whichever assets in whatever amounts he or she deems necessary in order to take full advantage of current and future market trends. (Some asset allocation funds, however, may have restrictions on amounts placed in the different markets. Make sure you know which one you are buying.)

Balanced mutual funds are affected by interest-rate changes, stock-market performance, and economic outlook. But by investing in a combination of stocks, bonds, and money-market instruments, true balanced funds are considerably less volatile than funds that invest solely in the stock market. The average volatility rating for Canadian balanced funds is 2.6, compared to 3.5 for equity funds.

Balanced Fund Returns

The average return for Canadian balanced funds over the five-year period to December 31, 1995, was 10.5%, and returns ranged from a high of 17.5% to a low of 7.1% — a difference of 10.4%. Interest and dividends are usually paid quarterly and capital gains annually. All Canadian balanced funds are RRSP eligible.

Finally, if it's a balanced fund you want, make sure that's what you get. Look under "Investment Objectives" in the fund prospectus. If that does not give enough detail, look at the fund's annual report for the current asset mix. This will give you, in percentages, the amounts placed in each market. If you are still not sure, call the fund company and ask if the fund has any restrictions on the amounts being invested: could the fund end up holding mostly bonds or stocks?

Key Points to Remember

- Balanced funds are a good "first" fund.
- They provide both growth and income in one fund.
- They are less volatile than equity funds.
- If it's a balanced fund you want, make sure that's what you get.

13

Specialized Funds

The following types of funds provide more investment opportunities geared to meet special needs or specific investment goals.

Dividend Funds

Many Canadian corporations pay a portion of their annual profits to shareholders in the form of dividend income. Dividend mutual funds invest in dividend-paying preferred shares of these corporations, and in common shares that are expected to yield a high level of dividend income.

Investors who purchase dividend funds receive a regular stream of income, usually monthly. Since some funds make distributions less frequently, you should investigate this before you buy if it is important for you to receive more regular payments. As with equity funds, there is also the potential for long-term capital growth through higher share prices of the fund's holdings. As dividend income is taxed at a much lower rate than other types of investment income, these funds are generally held outside of a registered plan.

To maximize the dividend tax credit, look for a mutual fund that holds most of its assets in preferred shares and high-yielding common stocks. If you normally invest in GICs but are considering a dividend fund, you may feel more secure investing in a fund with at least a P-2 rating (P-1 is the highest credit rating issued by the

Canadian Bond Rating Service and Dominion Bond Rating Service, P-2 next). Also, keep in mind that if you buy units in a dividend fund and then place them in your RRSP or RRIF, you negate the benefits of this tax credit.

Index Funds

The objective of an index fund is to mirror the performance of a benchmark, such as the TSE 300 Index, by investing in the same securities. If the index rises 14% in a year, an index fund will rise to nearly 14%. If the index falls 14%, an index fund will fall a little more than 14%. The fact that this type of fund does not increase as much and falls further than its benchmark is due to management fees. Therefore, the higher the fees, the greater the difference. Because managing an index fund requires no research or stock picking, there is little justification for high management fees. Look for a no-load index fund with the lowest management fees.

Special Equity Funds

These funds focus exclusively on specific industries and sectors of the economy and invest in companies in specialized areas such as real estate, resources, or precious metals. Given the cyclical nature of these industries (industries that are particularly sensitive to swings in economic conditions), special equity funds are the most volatile of all mutual funds. Some have a volatility rating of 9. Bear in mind that 10 is as high as you can go. Returns tend to fluctuate widely on an annual basis, which may mean posting a return of 85% one year and -14% the next. For investors who are willing to tolerate the volatility associated with these funds, the pay-off can be handsome. But losses, unfortunately, can be ugly. The experienced investor will have, at most, a small percentage of his or her portfolio invested in these funds. Remember: you are investing, not gambling!

Precious Metals Funds. These special equity funds invest in precious metals such as gold, silver, platinum, palladium, and rhodium and also in shares of mining exploration and production companies. Many financial planners recommend that investors keep 5% of their assets in this type of fund as a hedge against inflation. But because gold and other precious metals are subject to sudden and significant price movements, investment in this type of fund should be considered highly speculative. Although these funds offer investors the potential for substantial gains, there is also the possibility of considerable loss. Any capital gains are paid annually or can be reinvested in additional fund units.

Resource Funds. These funds invest in securities of Canadian companies involved in metals and minerals, oil and gas, forestry products, and water resources. Some also invest in precious metals. Again, returns will be volatile. Any capital gains are paid annually or can be reinvested in additional fund units.

Real-Estate Funds. Real-estate funds invest in commercial and industrial real estate. Returns are generated by the income from these investments, that is, rental and leasing, and potential capital gains — selling the properties for a profit. The attraction of this type of fund is the tax-sheltered rental income, so the fund is best kept outside of a registered plan. Due to the slump in real estate in the late 1980s, these funds have not fared well.

Moreover, units in some real-estate funds are not as easy to redeem as units in other types of mutual funds. A fund must have its properties appraised before the fund's assets can be valued and the unit price established. Appraisals are done quarterly or monthly, at which time you can get your money out. Income from real-estate funds is distributed quarterly and any capital gains annually.

Closed-End Funds

Like Canadian mutual funds, closed-end funds combine investors' money in a diversified portfolio of securities. But there the similarities end. Unlike open-ended mutual funds, the focus of this book, which create new shares based on investor demand, closed-end funds begin business with a fixed number of shares. The original sale of these shares is called an initial public offering (IPO). After this issue is sold, the shares are traded on major stock exchanges like regular shares of common stock.

The most important difference between a mutual fund and a closed-end fund is how the unit price is set. The unit price of a mutual fund is its net asset value — the value of the fund's holdings, less liabilities, divided by the number of shares outstanding. Since shares of closed-end funds are traded on the stock exchange, their price is set by supply and demand. They can trade for more (sell at a premium) or less (sell at a discount) than their net asset value.

Selecting a closed-end fund is much like choosing a mutual fund. Match the fund's objectives and risk levels with your own. It rarely makes sense, however, to buy a new issue of closed-end funds (unless they offer unusual investment opportunities), since they are usually offered at a high premium. Wait until the shares begin trading to buy them, usually at a discount.

Closed-end funds cannot be cashed in on demand like mutual funds, and in a declining market, finding buyers may prove difficult.

Segregated Funds

A segregated fund is a mutual fund offered by a life insurance company. The assets of the fund are segregated — hence the name — from the other assets of the company. Unlike mutual funds that are not protected by insurance, a segregated fund may guarantee that at maturity, or on your death, you, or your estate, will receive not less than 75%, and sometimes 100%, of the total amount originally invested. This means if you put in $10,000, you are guaranteed to receive at least $7,500. Sales commissions for segregated funds are usually non-negotiable. Also, life insurance funds offered through subsidiaries, rather than the life insurance company itself, may not be segregated and as such will not be guaranteed.

Key Points to Remember

- Dividend funds provide additional income.
- With special equities, a little should do you.
- Precious metals provide a hedge against inflation.
- Segregated funds are guaranteed.
- Index funds should have low management fees.

14

Investing Overseas

With Canada representing less than 3% of the world's stocks and bonds, it makes very little sense to ignore the tremendous investment opportunities in the global marketplace. That would be like doing all your grocery shopping at the corner store. Sure, it is convenient and familiar, but it does not stretch your dollar very far. By shopping for securities worldwide, you effectively stretch those investment dollars. Until the advent of mutual funds, however, these markets were out of reach to many investors.

Over the past few years, the number of international mutual funds has mushroomed in Canada, from less than 50 in 1985 to nearly 500 in 1995, as mutual fund companies tempt investors with the promise of higher returns in a variety of marketplaces. These include funds that offer high-interest income with the potential for capital growth and currency gains, and funds that offer the opportunity for higher long-term returns through wider diversification in international equities. Investors can now take their pick from funds with assets in a particular region, such as Europe, Asia, or the Pacific Rim, or a particular country, like China or the United States.

Although most commonly referred to as international funds, these funds fall into two different categories. International funds invest worldwide, excluding Canada. Global funds, on the other hand, invest around the world, including Canada.

Benefits of Investing Abroad

By now, you know that one of the major advantages of investing in mutual funds is diversification. By diversifying, you reduce risk, and by diversifying *worldwide*, you reduce that risk further. World markets do not all march to the beat of the same drummer. By investing in equity funds that hold assets in various countries or regions, you can take advantage of these different market timings. While Canadian markets may be performing poorly, overseas markets may be booming. Let's say you invest $20,000 solely in Canadian equities and the market declines 20%. You suffer a capital loss of $4,000. If instead you invest $16,000 in Canada and $4,000 in overseas equities, your capital loss is only $3,200, and any gains in overseas markets will reduce this loss further.

Moreover, returns on the Toronto Stock Exchange over the past ten years have never been at the top of the leader board. While we have been congratulating ourselves on returns of over 30% in 1993, stock markets in Germany, Norway, the United Kingdom, Brazil, Hong Kong, and Singapore significantly outperformed the Toronto Stock Exchange's 300 Composite Index — in some cases by as much as 100%.

The Added Risks

Investing internationally is not without its potential pitfalls. International funds are affected by the same risks as Canadian mutual funds and, in addition, are also sensitive to currency-exchange factors. When the Canadian dollar goes down in value against a country your fund holds assets in, you gain. When the Canadian dollar goes up in value against a country your fund holds assets in, you lose. If your overseas fund gains 15% but the Canadian dollar goes up in value against that currency by 10%, your actual gain will be (very roughly speaking) reduced to 5%. Moreover, if the Canadian dollar goes up in value and the markets in the country of investment are declining, you will take a double whammy. How successful a fund manager is in managing these different factors will have a direct effect on your returns.

The Different Types of International Funds

Like their domestic counterparts, funds that invest overseas fall into three main categories: money-market, bond, and equity.

International Money-Market Funds. These funds, like their Canadian counterparts, invest in high-quality and highly liquid short-term (maturing in less than one year) money-market securities issued by governments, financial institutions, and blue-chip corporations. While the majority focus on the U.S. money market, a few spread their wings and invest in short-term securities globally. Investing in international money-market funds provides investors with the opportunity to take advantage of higher interest rates elsewhere and serve as a hedge against a drop in value of the Canadian dollar.

To see how this works, assume that C$1 = US$0.80 and you purchase units in a U.S. money-market fund worth US$500. The cost to you will be C$625. If the Canadian dollar falls to US$0.70, and you decide to sell, you will receive C$714.29, for a capital gain of C$89.29 plus any accrued interest. Of course, if the Canadian dollar strengthens against the U.S. dollar, and now C$1 = US$0.90, you will receive only C$555.55, and incur a capital loss of C$69.44. Any interest earned will help offset this loss. U.S. money-market funds also provide investors with ready access to U.S. dollars.

Returns on these funds tend to cluster in a narrow band, with at most a one-percentage-point spread between the fund with the highest return and the one with the lowest. Clearly, no-load U.S. money-market funds with the lowest management expenses will have the edge.

For investors who wish to venture further afield, there are a few funds that invest in interest-bearing securities denominated in a variety of currencies such as the British pound, the French franc, and the German Deutschmark. Diversifying in this way reduces the risk inherent in investing in only one country and currency.

Interest income from international money-market funds is usually distributed monthly or can be automatically reinvested in additional fund units. By investing in Canadian short-term debt that is denominated in foreign currencies, several international money-market funds are 100% RRSP eligible. The remainder are eligible only to the current 20% foreign-content limit.

International Bond Funds. The primary objective of international bond funds is to provide a combination of fixed income and the opportunity for capital appreciation by investing selectively in government and corporate bonds worldwide. These funds seek opportunities around the world by investing in countries where interest rates are high and in those where there is the prospect of capital appreciation due to falling interest rates. (See Chapter 9 for more on bonds and interest rates.)

Unlike Canadian bond funds, these funds are denominated in foreign currencies and are subject to currency risk. This means that if the Canadian dollar falls against the other currencies contained in the fund portfolio, the value of the foreign bonds rises in terms of the dollar. As a result, the fund realizes a capital gain, which boosts its total rate of return. For example, if a bond fund earns £100 (100 pounds sterling), and assuming C$1 = £0.50, you make a capital gain of C$200. If, however, the Canadian dollar rises in value, and C$1 = £0.75, the fund experiences a capital loss. Your £100 is now worth only C$133.33.

Like their Canadian counterparts, international bond funds are interest-rate sensitive. When interest rates are rising in the country or region your fund holds assets in, bond prices drop. Conversely, when interest rates are falling, bond prices rise. For international bond funds, the best-case scenario is falling interest rates in the country of investment and a falling Canadian dollar. You'll be smiling all the way to the bank! The flip side is, of course, that if interest rates are rising in the country of investment, and the Canadian dollar also rises in value, the value of your investment may fall dramatically.

The average return for international bond funds over the five-year period to December 31, 1995, was 9.5%, and returns ranged from a high of 11.1% to a low of 8.3% — a difference of 2.8%.

Enthusiasm for international bond funds has grown dramatically in recent years. To give you an idea of the number of investment dollars we are talking about, there were only five funds before 1990, managing about $100 million in assets, but by 1995 this figure had soared to over $5 billion.

International Equity Funds. Typically, assets in international equity funds are invested in shares of companies in both the developed economies of North America and Europe and also the rapidly developing countries, also known as emerging markets, of Southeast Asia, Latin America, and Africa. Regardless of where they invest, the primary objective of these funds, like their Canadian counterparts, is to provide investors with long-term capital appreciation.

Returns on these funds will be affected by factors such as market conditions, political uncertainties in the country or region of investment, and exchange-rate fluctuations. The value of many of these funds may fluctuate widely and it is important to be aware of this before you buy. Emerging markets can quickly turn into "submerging markets." International and global funds spread their risk, however, by diversifying investments on a worldwide basis. This way, they are able to take advantage of high-growth regions as well as exploit the timing of stock-market cycles in different countries. As a result, these funds tend to be less volatile than international equity funds that invest in one country or region of the world. The majority of these funds are RRSP eligible up to the current 20% foreign-content limit.

The average return for international equity funds over the five-year period to December 31, 1995, was

12.9%, and returns ranged from a high of 23.9% to a low of 4.0% — a difference of 19.9%.

International Balanced Funds. The aim of these funds is to provide long-term capital growth plus regular income by investing in a combination of stocks, bonds, and short-term securities in different countries and industries around the world. A typical asset mix of 60% bonds and 40% stocks would change according to market conditions and the preferences of the portfolio manager. Generally speaking, international balanced funds are less volatile than international equity funds but more volatile than international money-market funds.

The average return for international balanced funds over the five-year period to December 31, 1995, was 10.8%, and returns ranged from a high of 14.6% to a low of 3.8% — a difference of 10.8%.

A Final Word

Investing worldwide provides investors with additional diversification, a hedge against a decline in the Canadian dollar, and the opportunity to take advantage of different market timings. Investors should, however, be aware of the exchange-rate risks and the volatility in returns associated with many of these funds. Moreover, management expenses are higher for international funds, due to the added cost of having overseas advisers and operating in foreign markets.

Key Points to Remember
- Going global adds diversification.
- Investing internationally decreases risk.
- International funds provide a hedge against a drop in the Canadian dollar.
- Be aware of exchange-rate risks.
- Emerging markets can turn into "submerging markets."

3
GETTING STARTED

15

Setting and Achieving Financial Objectives

Before investing in anything, let alone mutual funds, it is very important to take some time to reflect on where you are at this very moment financially: how much you own (your assets) less how much you owe (your liabilities). This financial snapshot is your "net worth." Assets might include cash held in a savings account, Canada Savings Bonds, GICs, bonds, stocks, mutual funds, pensions, property such as your home or cottage, cars, boats, and antiques. Liabilities might include a mortgage, loan, any unpaid bills, and the balance on your credit cards.

In addition, you need to get a handle on how much you can realistically invest. To arrive at this figure, deduct your total monthly expenses (such as rent or mortgage payments, insurance costs, car, parking, groceries, clothing, and entertainment) from your monthly net earnings. What you have left is the amount available for investment. For an annual figure, simply multiply by twelve. Of course, in many cases, there won't be anything left after you have paid all your bills. That's why many people pay themselves first. It is not easy, because you have to budget, but it is the most effective way to realize your financial goals.

Know Your Financial Objectives

When setting financial goals, you must be as specific as possible. Many people invest their money with at best only a vague idea of their financial objectives. "I want to save more money" is not a financial goal. Do you want to accumulate $500, $50,000, or $500,000? You must specify how much is "more," what it is going to be used for, and when you are going to need it. "I'd like to save money for a down payment on a house" is not specific enough. "I'd like to save $20,000 in ten years for a down payment on a house" is much better. You can then figure out if this is a realistic goal given the amount you have available for investing, your present financial situation, and your future prospects. If it is not, don't feel downhearted. You may have to do some fine-tuning. Perhaps, you could increase your investment amount by cutting back on one or more of your monthly expenses. Other options might include lengthening the investment time frame, or opting for a less expensive house. There are many roads to the same financial objective. It is not so much which one you take, only that you arrive — and arrive safely.

Financial objectives can range from building an emergency cash fund, to saving for your child's education, to retiring to a villa on a tropical island. Take the time *now* to really think about what you would like to achieve. Here are a few ideas to get you started (The possibilities are limitless, however):

> Additional current income — further education — emergency cash fund — vacations — down payment on a home — retirement income — child's education — vacation home — home renovation — automobile — round-the-world cruise — wedding expenses — cosmetic surgery — recreational vehicle — buy a franchise — start your own business — forty-foot motor cruiser — ???

How Much Is Enough?

Many people have no idea of how much money they need to invest to meet their financial objectives. Is $50 a month enough? Or would $300 be more appropriate?

ANNUAL INVESTMENT	RATE OF RETURN	GROWS TO AMOUNT INDICATED WITHIN					
		5 YEARS	10 YEARS	15 YEARS	20 YEARS	30 YEARS
$1,000	6%	5,975	13,972	24,673	38,993	83,802
	8%	6,336	15,645	29,324	49,423	122,346
	10%	6,716	17,531	34,950	63,002	180,943
	12%	7,115	19,655	41,753	80,699	270,293
	14%	7,536	22,045	49,980	103,768	406,737
$2,500	6%	14,938	34,929	61,681	97,482	209,504
	8%	15,840	39,114	73,311	123,557	305,865
	10%	16,789	43,828	87,374	157,506	452,359
	12%	17,788	49,136	104,383	201,747	675,732
	14%	18,839	55,111	124,951	259,421	1,016,843
$5,000	6%	29,877	69,858	123,363	194,964	419,008
	8%	31,680	78,227	146,621	247,115	611,729
	10%	33,578	87,656	174,749	315,012	904,717
	12%	35,576	98,273	208,766	403,494	1,351,463
	14%	37,678	110,223	249,902	518,842	2,033,685

Note: The amounts indicated assume reinvestment of all earnings and do not take into account any taxes.

The preceding table will give you a good fix on how much you will have to save each year over different time frames and with various returns to reach your desired goal.

As you can see from the table, if you invest $1,000 a year for thirty years, assuming an average rate of return of 10%, you will accumulate roughly $181,000. That's about $151,000 more than you put in. To harness the power of compound rates of return, increase that annual investment to $5,000. In thirty years, you will have amassed close to one million dollars — on a total investment of $150,000!

For a quick estimate of how much any investment will return, use the rule of 72. Simply divide 72 by the quoted return and you get a rough indication of how many years it will take for your money to double. This means $10,000 invested at 10% will double to $20,000 in just over seven years (72 divided by 10). At 7%, it will double in about ten years; at 15%, in around five years.

Identifying Appropriate Funds

Many people find it difficult to identify which funds best meet their financial objectives. The following quiz will help you make a start. Answer the questions honestly and then add up the stars. It is especially important not to fool yourself when it comes to the amount of risk you are comfortable with. If preserving your money — not exposing it to any risk — is your number one concern, or if you have an investment time frame of less than five years, then your risk level can only be "low."

INVESTMENT PROFILE QUIZ

Age?	50 & over* ❐	35–50** ❐	20–35*** ❐
When will you need your money?	1–5 years* ❐	5–10 years** ❐	10 years & ❐ up***

How much risk are you comfortable with?	Low* ❏	Moderate** ❏	High*** ❏

Financial objectives?	Safety of Capital/ ❏ Income*	Income/ Growth** ❏	Maximum Growth*** ❏

Scores will range from a low of four stars — for cautious or short-term investors who do not want to put their capital (the initial amount invested) at risk — to a high of twelve stars — for the more aggressive or longer-term investor who is willing to accept a higher degree of risk in order to achieve maximum growth. Generally speaking, therefore, the lower your score, the more income funds, the lower the growth potential, and the lower the volatility. The higher your score, the more equity funds, the higher the return potential, and the higher the volatility.

Building a Core Portfolio

Many financial experts recommend building a core investment portfolio of the following:

- a money-market fund, T-bill fund, and/or savings account (as an emergency cash fund if you don't already have one)
- a good-quality bond fund and/or GICs
- an equity fund that holds assets in well-established Canadian companies, and an international equity fund

Younger, more aggressive, or wealthier investors could include the more volatile special equity, Asian, or emerging-markets funds. Moreover, if you are in a higher tax bracket, you might want to consider adding a Canadian dividend fund. If you want to keep it simple, or have limited investment dollars, pick a Canadian balanced fund and add an international equity fund later.

Asset Allocation

How you divide your money among the different asset classes in your investment portfolio is called "asset allocation." For example, scoring twelve stars in the investment profile quiz does not mean you should place *all* of your money in equity mutual funds. It simply means that your asset allocation should place a larger percentage in equity funds than for someone who scores, say, eight stars.

The following asset allocation chart is at best only a guide. You should seek out additional help (see Chapter 17) to determine the right combination of funds that are suitable for you.

ASSET ALLOCATION CHART

	Cash or Equivalent	Income	Growth
4–6 stars	10%–30%	50%–70%	10%–30%
7–9 stars	0%–20%	40%–60%	40%–60%
10–12 stars	0%–20%	20%–40%	50%–80%

There is no one "best" asset allocation. For example, a young couple planning to buy a home within the next three to five years should not put their capital at risk by investing solely in equity funds. They may need their money when the stock market is down. Instead, their investment portfolio could look like this:

30% — Savings account and/or Canadian money-
  market funds
60% — GICs and/or income funds
10% — Canadian equity funds

On the other hand, an older couple (but still many years away from retirement) with no mortgage, and children who are now self-sufficient, may want to take advantage of this period to boost their retirement savings. In this case, the following asset allocation may be more appropriate:

10% — Savings account and/or Canadian money-
        market funds
30% — GICs and/or income funds
60% — Equity funds (including international)

Many of you may already hold investments that fit into one or another of these asset classes. If, for example, you own Canada Savings Bonds or cashable GICs, then you can divide your mutual fund investments between income and growth. If you are still unsure, and have an investment time frame of at least five years, use the following highly sophisticated method: subtract your age from 100; the difference is the percentage you should consider putting in equities!

Most banks and trust companies have worksheets to help you zero in on asset allocation. Some are extremely user-friendly and will take at the most five or ten minutes to complete; others are more complex. Even if one of the staff explains the form to you, or helps you complete it, there is absolutely no obligation on your part to buy any of the products being sold.

Rebalancing Your Investment Portfolio

You should set aside time at least once annually to review your investment portfolio. Whenever investment objectives are met, take the time to determine your new goals and invest accordingly. Depending on your new objectives, this might mean only a slight adjustment to your portfolio or a major switch from one asset class to another.

You may also find that one asset class does very well and increases from, say, 40% to 60% of your investment portfolio. In that case, you should consider taking your profits and rebalancing back to your original asset allocation. Another option might be to put any new investment money into the other funds in your portfolio and hold off putting anything more into the fund that has grown. Chapter 20 — "How to Stay on Top" — highlights other important factors that you should consider.

A Final Word

Finances are no different from any other aspect of life. You must set goals and then actively work towards them. Visualizing a certain standard of living when you retire, or a new home with a 150-foot lot, is merely daydreaming unless you set up an action plan and start putting aside the money now.

Key Points to Remember

- Pay yourself first.
- Set specific financial goals.
- Asset allocation means how you divide your money up.
- There is no "best" asset allocation.
- Review your holdings periodically.

16

The Seven Steps to Successful Investing

Most people would never dream of walking into a travel agency to buy their annual vacation without first having a good idea of where they wanted to go, and how and when they wanted to get there. Yet, when it comes to purchasing mutual funds for their financial future, a surprising number of people do just that. Is it any wonder that they end up not only frustrated and unhappy with their investments but sometimes also extremely nervous? For some, it is like ending up on a heli-ski vacation when their idea of excitement is to lie in the sun and play an occasional round of mini-golf!

Before you start buying units in a mutual fund, you should first complete the following seven steps:

Step 1 — Know your financial goals. Where are you going? What is your time frame? How much will you need?

Step 2 — Identify suitable funds. Should you invest in income funds? Or growth funds? Are you comfortable with wide swings in return or would you prefer more stable returns?

Step 3 — Determine your asset allocation. What is the right combination of funds for you? Is 60% in equities too much? Or too little?

Step 4 — Make a shortlist of two or three suitable funds within your selected categories. To do this, compare returns, MERs, volatility ratings, and sales commissions. See Chapter 18, "Doing Your Homework."

Step 5 — Call the mutual fund companies and request a prospectus and annual report. Read both carefully. Double-check that the objective and risk level match your own. Chapter 19 highlights the important points.

Step 6 — Select the most suitable fund(s) within each category. Before purchasing, always check current performance figures. Specifically, you need to know whether the fund is still producing above-average returns for its category and make sure there has been no recent change of management.

Step 7 — Stay on top of your investments. Monitoring your funds' returns on a monthly basis puts you in the driver's seat. Chapter 20 shows you how.

17

Shopping Around for the Best Advice

If you are unsure of any step in Chapter 16, you can get advice from many different sources such as your local bank or trust company, brokers, and financial planners. Don't be surprised, however, if they ask a lot of personal questions. They should. One of the principal securities regulations affecting companies that sell securities is called the "know-your-client rule." This states that in order for securities dealers to act in the best interests of their clients, they must understand their clients' financial objectives and the level of risk they are comfortable with. Dealers may do this by asking numerous questions relating to your personal finances (such as family income, debt obligations, investments), comfort level, and investment experience. This is not idle curiosity. They need this information in order to advise you which are the best investments for you personally. If they *don't* ask any questions, you should think twice before investing in the funds they recommend.

Seek referrals from friends and colleagues wherever possible, but remember, whoever you choose should be able to provide you with easy-to-understand answers to all your questions, make specific recommendations to fit your investment goals, and explain the risks.

Financial Planners. Make sure they are accredited either as a Registered Financial Planner or as a Chartered Financial Planner. Some charge an hourly fee to develop a financial plan and do not sell financial products such as mutual funds. Others charge a fee for a financial plan plus a commission for any investment purchased, or provide the plan free if you buy your investments through that person. Ask what the fees will be, what services they provide, and what products they sell. Bear in mind that financial planners who rely on sales commissions from the investment products they sell may be biased towards load funds.

Full-Service Brokers. Most communities have at least one storefront broker's office. Wander in (you don't have to be dressed up — casual clothes are just fine) and pick up some information sheets on the services they provide. Brokers, licensed by the province they practise in, can advise you on a very broad range of investments such as stocks, bonds, stripped bonds, GICs, and mutual funds. Brokers do not receive a salary but rather make their living through the commissions on the investment products they sell. For this reason, they may be biased towards load funds and fund companies that pay high trailer fees or provide other incentives. A handling fee of between $50 and $100, depending on the amount being invested, may be charged on the purchase of no-load funds.

Bank-Owned Brokers provide the same services as full-service brokers. Their marketing push may, however, be towards selling the investment products (such as mutual funds) of their parent company.

Discount Brokers offer the same selection of investment products as full-service brokers. But because you receive little or no investment advice, the sales commission for purchasing a load fund is generally 1% for amounts over $25,000 and 2% for amounts under. Some discount brokers charge 2.5% for amounts up to $5,000.

If you choose the back-end load option, the fees charged by individual mutual fund companies will apply. When you purchase a no-load fund, a fee of around $40 is usually charged. Most major banks have a discount brokerage arm.

Investment Counsellors manage your money but generally only if you have large amounts to manage. The fee payable is usually a percentage of the assets of your investment portfolio.

Chartered Accountants focus on specific areas such as tax or estate planning, although some are also financial planners. Most charge a set or hourly fee.

Banks and Trust Companies. Probably the most user friendly, they have plenty of free parking and investment advice. Moreover, recognizing a need, most financial institutions are now upgrading the training requirements for their investment advisers. Financial institutions also offer free information kits and seminars on all aspects of personal finance. Some provide complimentary videos on topics such as RRSPs. However, banks and trust companies will offer only their own family of funds. The only exception to date is the Toronto Dominion Bank, which plans to offer third-party funds from four or five well-known mutual fund companies.

Mutual Fund Companies and Insurance Companies. The advice is free but, in the case of individual mutual fund companies, will vary depending on the level of expertise of the individual. Most have good information packages, which you can obtain by calling their toll free number. Again, your choice of funds will be limited to within their particular mutual fund family.

A Final Word

If you feel pressured or doubtful about the advice given, try somewhere else. In fact, it is a good idea to shop around two or three places. You will be amazed at how much additional information you can pick up. Your final choice should be a company or person that you feel confident and comfortable with. Don't rush. Remember, it is your money and your financial future. Moreover, while the advice being given on building an investment portfolio may be excellent, the funds recommended may not!

18

Doing Your Homework

There is no methodology that can unfailingly predict which mutual funds will perform well in the future. It doesn't matter which book, magazine, or newspaper you consult, which "expert" you listen to, or even which sophisticated computer software you use. Nevertheless, there are some relevant factors that can increase the likelihood of investing in a mutual fund that will provide above-average returns. Moreover, these factors will certainly decrease the possibility of investing in a poor performer.

Past Performance

Although — as all mutual fund advertisements clearly state — past performance is no indication of future performance, past performance is a good measure of how a fund has fulfilled its objectives. Moreover, past performance figures can steer you away from poor-performing funds. One of the simplest methods of screening the past performance of mutual funds is to look carefully at their annual compound rates of return over different time frames. These returns measure the average annual change in net asset value per share, assuming all dividends and capital gains are reinvested, but exclude sales or redemption charges. To review how returns are calculated, see Chapter 6.

What to Look For

You should concentrate your possible selection from funds that have consistently delivered above-average compound rates of return, *relative to similar funds*, over each one-year, three-year, and five-year period.[1] In other words, compare bond funds with bond funds, and Canadian equity funds with other Canadian equity funds, and zero in on the consistent top performers. The different time periods give a good indication of how a fund has performed under various market conditions. To look only at a five-year compound rate of return, for example, can be misleading. A fund may have done extremely well in any one of those five years but performed poorly in the other four. That one year's stellar performance could, however, easily boost the five-year compound return and give a misleading impression of the fund's performance. This screening process will also steer you clear of those funds that have consistently delivered below-average returns.

To illustrate why these comparisons are important, let's look at a typical mutual fund advertisement:

	RATE OF RETURN		
	1-YR	**3-YR**	**5-YR**
XYZ Int'l Equity Fund	9.76%	16.60%	11.30%

These figures by themselves won't tell you much unless you know the rates of return for all international equity funds over the same time periods. For example, if the average rates of return for international equity funds were 7%, 12.50%, and 10% respectively, then the XYZ Fund was obviously an above-average performer in each and every time period. But suppose the average rates of return were 14%, 22.15%, and 16.50%. This puts the

---

[1] All "Heavy Hitters" — consistently above-average funds — are ranked in *Ranga Chand's World of Mutual Funds* (Stoddart Publishing), taking into account an appropriate benchmark, quartile performance, and volatility. That book also lists the "Underachievers" — the consistently below-average funds.

XYZ Fund's returns in a very different and unflattering light. Also, don't be sidetracked by being told that a fund outperformed the T-bill rate. While this is important information, it is not enough. You still need to know how the fund compares with its peers.

Narrowing Down the Choice

You will find there are many above-average-performing funds to choose from in each category. Therefore, in order to narrow down the choice, you should now look at their performance on a calendar year basis. Key factors to consider are:

Benchmark Performance. Comparing a fund's annual returns with an appropriate benchmark gives additional valuable information on that fund's performance. The most commonly used benchmarks are market indexes such as the TSE 300 Total Return Index (for Canadian equity funds). This index is a measurement of the general performance of a broad range of 300 stocks listed on the Toronto Stock Exchange. It includes changes in stock prices, plus the dividends earned by stocks in the index. Other indexes include the ScotiaMcLeod Universe Bond Index (for Canadian bond funds), the ScotiaMcLeod Conventional Mortgage Index (for short-term bond or mortgage funds), the S&P 500 (for U.S. equity funds), the Morgan Stanley World Index (for international equity funds), and the Morgan Stanley Europe, Australasia, Far East Index (EAFE) (for Asian funds). By comparing a Canadian equity fund with the TSE 300 Total Return Index, for example, you can see how often the fund has beaten this benchmark over the last five years. This allows you to judge the fund's performance during periods when the TSE was declining, as well as when it was increasing.

Quartile Performance. How often did a fund achieve either a first-quartile (top 25%) or a second-quartile (top 50%) performance in its category? This is additional information that will help in your selection process. Although it is rare for any fund to be in the top 25% year in, year out, many funds do achieve a first-quartile performance on a fairly regular basis.

Volatility. As investors, we are all interested in the question of risk and whether the risk is worth the reward. Given the choice, most investors would prefer to receive superior returns with lower risk. Therefore, you should target the above-average-performing funds with the lowest volatility ratings.

You should also compare additional factors such as management styles, sales commissions, and management expenses. Obviously, a no-load fund that meets all the above requirements with below-average management fees would be perfect. Realistically, finding such a fund may not always be possible. Your final selection process will to a large extent be governed by your personal criteria. Bear in mind that it is not always the top-performing fund that will best meet your own specific needs.

A Final Word

Aggressive marketing or a seemingly authoritative sales pitch can and does influence even the most seasoned investors. It is easy to be impressed by a fund's 36% return, enticed by the prospects of a booming overseas economy, or overwhelmed and confused by technical jargon. Don't react. Act in your own best interests. Evaluate each fund on its own merits, and above all, compare its returns to similar funds and to an *appropriate* benchmark. If it is a load fund and seems like a good investment, you may want to consider looking for a comparable no-load fund instead. If none exists, or if you feel you need the ongoing help of a financial adviser, perhaps paying the sales commission is justified.

19

The Prospectus

All mutual fund companies must provide all prospective investors with an up-to-date copy of their mutual funds' simplified prospectus. Of course, companies have no way of ensuring that you read it. If you don't, or merely give it a token glance, you could be in for some very nasty surprises further down the road. This document, although not exactly user friendly, is a must-read. Unlike the glossy marketing brochures, which tend to dwell only on the positive, the prospectus gives you all the information you need to know about a fund's investment objectives, policies, fees, and the degree of potential risk in owning the fund's units.

Once you have received the prospectuses for the funds you are interested in, set aside twenty to thirty minutes and highlight with a magic marker the fund's objectives, degree of risk, and all the fees payable. This way, you will be able to compare these important points with similar funds. It also makes for a quick and easy reference if you require additional information or clarification from the mutual fund company or salesperson. Make sure the documents you receive are for the current year; the date is usually given on the front cover.

By regulation, prospectuses must summarize all fees and expenses in the first two pages. Although this is a useful guide, it is extremely important that you don't stop there. You must read the entire document to ensure that you fully understand a fund's fee structure.

Although there are no hidden fees, some charges are less apparent than others.

The important sections are as follows:

Investment Objectives. The information contained in this section will help you decide whether a fund's investment objectives match your own. Because of the financial jargon used, this is not always easy to determine. If you are not sure how to interpret the objectives of a fund, call your salesperson or the mutual fund company's toll free number. Unless you fully understand the fund's objectives, you cannot possibly match them to your own.

Fund Expenses. This section lists the management fee and the management expense ratio for each fund included in the prospectus. Although, as stated earlier, these fees are not negotiable, you should spend a few minutes reading this section to see what expenses are paid by the fund. Remember, *the higher the management expense ratio, the lower the returns to unitholders*. The management expense ratio will vary according to the type of fund, but generally equity funds will be at the high end (the average is about 2%) and money-market funds at the low end (averaging about 1%). Some prospectuses give the management expense ratio paid during the previous five years. Check for consistency: no dramatic increases.

Investors' Expenses. This section lists all the possible costs that could be incurred by investors, such as sales commissions and transfer, redemption, trailer, distribution, RRSP/RRIF, and set-up and closing fees. To refresh your memory on these and other expenses, turn back to Chapter 3, "How Much Will It Cost?"

Income from Mutual Funds. This tells you what distributions (income and capital gains) are paid and when. Most funds automatically reinvest any distributions unless they receive a written request specifying otherwise. If you would rather receive regular payments, make sure you fill in the necessary forms at the time of purchase.

Purchase of Units. This section tells you that units are offered for sale on a continuous basis at a price equal to their net asset value. This means if the NAV is, say, $13.50 on the day of purchase, then that is the price you will pay for every unit of the fund bought at that time. This section also tells you who you can purchase units from and how payment must be made.

Risk Factors. It is important that you read the risk section carefully. As well as informing unitholders that there is no guarantee that they will recover their original investment, it also details the specific risks, such as currency or interest rates, involved in investing in the various funds.

Income-Tax Considerations. The income-tax section details all payments — capital gains, dividends, and interest — made to unitholders and the subsequent tax implications. Unitholders should receive a T3 (from a mutual fund trust) or T5 (from a mutual fund corporation) slip each year, showing the exact amounts of each paid.

Registered Plans. This section gives details on which funds are fully eligible to be held in tax-sheltered plans such as RRSPs and RRIFs, and which funds are eligible only to the 20% foreign-content limit. It also gives the minimum initial contribution for each type of plan listed.

Redemption of Securities. The redemption section tells unitholders how they can redeem (sell back) their units to the fund, usually at the net asset value determined at close of trading on any valuation day (usually 4 p.m. Eastern Time). Redemption requests are generally required in writing, with the signature of the unitholder guaranteed by a bank, trust company, broker, or mutual fund salesperson.

Purchasers' Statutory Rights. Securities legislation provides purchasers with the right to withdraw from an agreement to purchase mutual funds within two business days after receiving the prospectus or within forty-eight hours after the receipt of a confirmation of purchase. Essentially, this legislation means that if you wake up the next morning and decide the fund you just bought is too risky or not a good match with your investment goals, you have the right to withdraw from the purchase and get your money back.

Annual Report. This report, which should come with the prospectus, gives a detailed list of all assets held in the various funds. Although some of these assets may have changed by the time you read the annual report, it will still give you a much better idea of whether or not the fund is compatible with your investment objectives and risk level. Instead of reading general descriptions such as "stocks of large Canadian companies," which tend to appear in the marketing brochures of many equity funds, you may find it interesting to see the names of the companies the fund actually invests in. Investing in a mutual fund also makes for more exciting reading in the business section of your newspaper. After all, once you purchase units in a fund, you will have a vested interest in how these companies are performing.

The annual report also includes a summary of each fund's performance and any changes in investment objectives, management fees, or responsibilities.

Key Points to Remember
- The prospectus is a must-read.
- The investment objectives and risk levels given should closely match your own.
- Double-check what fees are payable.
- Use the prospectus to comparison shop.
- Annual reports list assets held.

20

How to Stay on Top

When it comes to investing in mutual funds, many people misinterpret the phrase "long-term." Their investment philosophy may be best summed up as "Buy it and forget it." However, many factors can and do influence the performance of mutual funds, and if you decide to invest in them, you should be prepared to spend some time monitoring them. As little as half an hour each month could make all the difference in your returns.

What to Read

The *Globe and Mail's Report on Business*. The *Globe* publishes a special mutual funds section on the third Thursday of each month. It also publishes the net asset value for all mutual funds on a daily basis.

The *Financial Post*. Like the *Globe*, the *Post* publishes a monthly fund survey in their weekend issue dated the third Monday of each month.

The *Toronto Star*. The *Star* publishes a monthly fund survey in their weekend edition dated the second Sunday of each month.

By reading any of these monthly fund reports, you will be able to check on your fund's performance and how it is doing compared with similar funds. On a sheet of paper, write the year and the month and put down the monthly and one-year return for your fund and the average monthly and one-year return for that fund group. You should also compare your fund's return with its relative index. Try to do this every month. Over time, you will easily see if your fund is continuing to track above average or is on a downward trend. Keep these records in your mutual fund file or envelope.

Sometimes your fund will show a negative monthly return. Again, check the average. If your fund returned -1.3% but the average was -2.1%, your fund is still doing better. You should not be alarmed if your fund *occasionally* does slip below the average. This is normal. Moreover, if you have purchased units in a fund with a high volatility rating, you should expect wide swings in returns.

Investors who want the most up-to-date information in a disc format should consider BellCharts on Disk (tel: 416-515-4757), The Mutual Fund Sourcedisk (tel: 1-800-268-7742), or PALTrak for Windows (tel: 1-800-531-4725).

Mutual Fund Company Reports. These regularly issued reports give information on your fund's rate of return and any shifts in portfolio asset allocation. For example, in a Latin American fund, the manager may decide to hold more securities (increase the weighting) in Brazil and fewer securities in Argentina. These reports also include a detailed "Statement of Investment Portfolio" with the number and type of assets owned by the fund. Any changes in objectives, management fees, or responsibilities will also be included in this report.

Mutual Fund Company Statement of Account. This gives the current total value of your account and shows all transactions, including income and/or capital gains information. You should keep these statements in a file. That way, you can compare the latest total value given, unit price, etc., with the previous numbers.

What to Watch For

Declining Returns. You should regularly compare your fund's performance to the performance of similar funds. Most funds are going to have off periods. It is not the occasional downturn we are talking about, but rather a steady decline in performance. Don't confuse this with a bear market, when most if not all stocks or bonds will fall. What we are focusing on here is when the performance of your fund — be it equity or bond — continually falls below the average for its group over an extended period of time such as nine to twelve months. Once you have established a definite downward pattern that is not related to the market as a whole or the fund's normal volatility, hold off putting in any new money. If things don't improve, it may be time to move on.

Change in Management. This may or may not have an impact on the performance of your fund. Some funds are managed by teams, in which case one person leaving is usually of less consequence. In the case of a fund managed by "one person," you need to find out the track record and qualifications of the new manager, hold off putting any new money in, and keep a watchful eye on returns.

On the flip side, should you follow a manager from one company to another? First, you should bear in mind that any manager will have to put *their* stamp on the fund they are taking over. This may take some time, so there is no need to make a hasty decision. Second, it may be prudent not to invest large amounts until you see what sort of returns the fund is generating. There is no guarantee that a manager will be able to replicate their previous track record.

Since fund companies don't tend to advertise when a manager leaves, it is sometimes difficult to obtain this information. Ontario Securities Commissioner Glorianne Stromberg, in her "Mutual Fund Industry Review," has recommended changes to include advising investors in a timely fashion of any change in management.

Rebalancing. This is one of the most important and probably one of the most neglected steps. If you start with an asset allocation of, say, 50% equities and 50% bonds, then this should accurately reflect your financial objectives, return expectations, and risk tolerance. At the end of the year, if your equity funds have done really well, you may end up with 75% equities and 25% bonds. This asset allocation would be more suitable for an investor with a longer investment time frame or higher risk level. In order to avoid this situation, you should periodically review your asset allocation and rebalance to your original mix. Moreover, as your investment objectives change, so should your asset allocation.

The bottom line is that successful investing — much like everything else in life — requires effort. With mutual funds, however, a little effort can go a long way. By spending about half an hour a month now, you will be in a much better position further down the road to judge whether you should buy more units in a particular fund or sell the ones you already have.

Key Points to Remember

- Regularly compare your fund's performance with its peers'.
- Mutual fund company reports tell you what's happening with a fund.
- Statements of account tell you what's happening to the value of your investment.
- Watch for declining returns.
- Don't forget to rebalance.

21

Investment Strategies

Buy low and sell high. Sounds easy, but many people end up doing the exact opposite. They start off with the best of intentions but succumb to panic (when prices plummet, they sell) and greed (when prices soar, they hang on too long). This scenario is more true when investing in individual stocks than in mutual funds, but it doesn't exclude funds entirely — especially in the case of equity funds and, needless to say, when the markets take a roller-coaster ride.

Market Timing

Investors who pursue a market-timing approach, however, are not so concerned with getting in at rock-bottom prices or selling at the peak. Instead, their aim is to share in most of a bull market while escaping most of a decline. They try to invest in equity funds just before an economic recovery starts, move out before the peak, and move into bond funds just as the downturn begins. Of course, in reality, even though they may have judged the business cycle correctly, markets often move down when they are expected to move up and vice versa. Moreover, there are the added problems of either having too much invested in a particular market when it goes down or being out of a market when it goes up. Market timing is used at least to some extent by most individual investors and portfolio managers.

Dollar Cost Averaging

There are many market-timing approaches, but one of the simplest is "dollar cost averaging." This investment technique lends itself extremely well to mutual funds. By investing a fixed amount of money at regular intervals, you buy more units in a mutual fund when prices are down and fewer when prices are high. This reduces the average price per unit. The more frequently you invest, such as monthly rather than semi-annually, the greater your chances of buying units when prices are especially low. To see how this works, assume you invest $100 per month:

DATE	AMOUNT INVESTED	PRICE PER UNIT	UNITS BOUGHT	TOTAL UNITS
Jan 1	$100.00	$10.00	10	10
Feb 1	$100.00	$8.00	12.50	22.50
Mar 1	$100.00	$12.50	8	30.50
Apr 1	$100.00	$11.50	8.70	39.20

After four months, your $400 has bought you 39.20 units at an average price of $10.20 per unit. Some of you no doubt are staring fixedly at the $8 price per unit. Yes, if you had bought at that particular time and had the $400 to spare, you would have received 50 units. But with the unit price so low, you might have stayed on the sidelines, wondering if it was going to fall further. On the other hand, you might have jumped in and bought in March when unit prices were $12.50, anxious not to miss out on what looked like a good thing, and purchased only 26.67 units. As you can see, dollar cost averaging eliminates any emotional investment decisions and reduces the average cost of your investments over time. Many people use this investment strategy without being aware of it. If, for example, you pay a fixed amount monthly into a company pension plan, or reinvest fund distributions (even though the amounts may vary), you are already dollar cost averaging!

If you are just getting started in mutual funds, or have limited amounts to invest, dollar cost averaging has many additional advantages. It doesn't require large amounts of money, and it forces you to stick to a financial plan. Most financial institutions and mutual fund companies allow you to invest as little as $25 a month in a pre-authorized investment plan. The money is withdrawn automatically from your bank account and invested in the funds of your choice.

Buy and Hold

This is probably the most common strategy used by mutual fund investors and involves no complicated methodology. A buy and hold strategy works especially well with equity funds. As stated earlier, although their returns tend to be more volatile in the short term, historically they have provided a higher average rate of return over the longer term. It does, however, require a prudent appraisal of the markets and funds before investing. For example, it would be unwise to invest a large amount of money in an equity fund if the stock-market is at an all-time high and is poised for a correction, or in a bond fund if interest rates are headed up. If you are unsure, put your money into a Canadian money-market fund and use dollar cost averaging. That way, you will be in a good position to take advantage of investment opportunities when the market settles.

Buy and hold does not mean that you should never sell. If your investment objectives change, your asset allocation, and perhaps some of the funds themselves, may no longer be appropriate. Moreover, you should probably consider moving on if a fund has consistently delivered below-average returns over an extended period of time. Any deferred sales charges payable on redeeming any or all of your units should be factored into your decision.

The buy and hold strategy should not be confused with the "buy it and forget it" philosophy. With the former, you regularly review your investments and make decisions accordingly. With the latter, you do absolutely nothing. Although in the short term this may appeal to those of us who can't be bothered and would rather leave it all to someone else, you may find over the longer term that your returns are on a par with your personal involvement!

Asset Allocation

This method of investing involves dividing your money among a variety of investments, thereby decreasing risk. In this way, if your bond fund performs poorly, your equity fund may do well. Moreover, when the Canadian economy goes into a recession, overseas markets may perform strongly. The general rule is that over time (at least five years), stocks do better than bonds and bonds do better than cash.

Don't make the mistake of thinking that just because you hold units in five or six mutual funds, you are already using this investment strategy. You may have a complete hodgepodge, having bought units in each new "hot" fund as it hit the market. Holding many funds is not asset allocation unless some thought has been given to how the funds complement each other.

Many financial institutions and mutual fund companies offer asset allocation mutual funds. Some of these funds, however, may hold a higher percentage of stocks than you would be comfortable with (see Chapter 12).

A Final Word

Deciding on an investment strategy may have a lot more appeal to many people than working on their investment objectives. But for any investment plan to work, and work well, you must first define your investment goals. This is the first step, and without taking it you are likely to trip up.

Key Points to Remember
- Investment objectives are the first step.
- Market timing is extremely difficult.
- Dollar cost averaging reduces the average price per unit.
- Buy and hold does not mean forever.
- Asset allocation decreases risk.

22

Common Investment Mistakes and How to Avoid Them

Procrastination. The more you delay, the less money you will accumulate and the less chance you will have of achieving your financial objectives. Take a sheet of paper and write down what your goals are and how much money you can realistically set aside each month to achieve them. Do it now. Once any goal is written down, you have made your first step in the right direction. It doesn't matter if it is $25 or $500 a month. If you don't get started, it will end up the same — a big fat zero!

Investing in Inappropriate Funds. To avoid investing in unsuitable funds, you must have a good understanding of your investment objectives and the level of risk you are willing to tolerate to achieve them. Someone else's "best buy" could be your worst nightmare.

Buying a "Hot" Fund. Returns of 46% or 65% tend to get a lot of media and marketing hype. While the fund may indeed have impressive one-year returns, this is in itself no reason to buy. These returns are history. Only the people already invested in the fund will have reaped the rewards. Is the fund invested in a region, country, or sector that is expected to perform well over the longer term? What kind of performance history does it have? Does it generate equally dramatic negative returns? Is it a suitable fund for your investment objectives and risk level? Who is promoting it and why? These are the kind of questions you should be seeking answers to — before you buy.

Investing in Only One Market. By putting all of your investment dollars into one market, you run the risk that if it performs badly you will lose money. Investors who diversify by holding funds in different markets (money-market, bonds, and stocks) and different countries tend to reduce risk and generate higher returns over the longer term. If one market or country is in a slump, another may be booming.

Unrealistic Expectations. Many investors base their financial plans on achieving repeated annual returns of 20% or 25%. Over the past ten years, the average annual return from mutual funds for Canadian bonds was 11.4%, Canadian equities 10.4%, and Asian funds 16.5%. Clearly, to expect a return of over 20% year after year is unrealistic, and any investment plan based on this expectation is doomed to fail. Make sure your investment goals are based on realistic returns.

Not Keeping Records. It is important to keep all confirmation statements that detail your purchases and redemptions, including units purchased when distributions are reinvested. You may need these statements for income-tax purposes.

Panic and Greed. These are two powerful emotions which often drive otherwise sensible people to make unwise investment decisions. First, returns on most funds will vary, and some will vary a lot more than others. If you do your homework before you buy, you will be aware of these fluctuations and will not be panic-driven to sell at the wrong time. Moreover, many investors, quite understandably, go into a tailspin when the market declines and rush to redeem their units. It is at this time, when prices are low, that the savvy investor hangs tough and buys additional units.

Second, to put most or all of your money into a highly volatile fund in the hope of making huge returns is not investing. It is gambling, or greed. Also, you may find yourself unable to cope should you have to sustain a large financial loss. By all means invest in some of the riskier funds, but do it with a full understanding of the risks involved, and preferably on the stingy side.

Buying Decisions Based on Newspaper Articles or Glossy Fund Brochures. Without doing your homework (see Chapter 18) and reading the prospectus, this could be a costly mistake. Let's face it, all mutual fund companies tend to emphasize the positive in their battle for your investment dollars. They may quote a seemingly impressive yearly return or five-year performance history. All this makes for good advertising. But unless you compare the numbers quoted with returns of similar funds over the same time frame, you have absolutely no idea whether the fund's performance was good, bad, or merely average. Moreover, many newspaper and magazine articles promote one fund over another. Never buy units in a fund based solely on these infomercials. It may not be in your best interests.

Glossary

Asset Anything having commercial or exchange value that is owned by a business, institution, or individual.

Asset Mix Assets are distributed among stocks, bonds, and money-market instruments (treasury bills, certificates of deposit, short-term government bonds, and commercial paper).

Back-End Load A charge for withdrawing shares from a mutual fund.

Balanced Mutual Fund An investment fund that usually includes bonds, debentures, or preferred shares, in varying ratios with common stocks.

Bear Market A prolonged period of falling prices. A bear market in stocks is usually brought on by the anticipation of declining economic activity, and a bear market in bonds is caused by rising interest rates.

Bond Mutual Fund An investment fund predominantly made up of bonds and debentures.

Bonds Certificates issued by borrowers, usually governments or corporations. A bond will normally have a fixed interest rate and a set maturity date, at which time the principal will be repaid in full. A typical bond will have interest coupons attached which are redeemed annually or semi-annually.

Broker A person who acts as an intermediary in the purchase of securities or insurance.

Bull Market A prolonged rise in the prices of stocks, bonds, or commodities. Bull markets may last from a few months to several years and are characterized by high trading volume.

Capital Cost Allowance A tax deduction for the depreciation of various types of assets.

Capital Gains The difference between the buy and sell price of an asset. The capital gain on stocks purchased for $1,000 and sold for $1,450 would be $450.

Closed-End Mutual Fund A fund in which the total number of shares is fixed. After the initial offer, the shares can be acquired only from another owner. Share prices are set by supply and demand, not net asset value, and are traded on a stock exchange.

Commercial Paper Short-term debt securities issued by corporations, banks, and other borrowers.

Common Share A security representing part ownership in a company, generally carrying the right to vote on major decisions and to receive dividends.

Coupons Certificates attached to a bond that can be redeemed for interest payments at regular intervals.

Debenture General debt obligation backed only by the integrity of the borrower. An unsecured bond is a debenture.

Deposit Insurance Protection of certain types of assets against loss. Bank and trust company deposits are covered by the Canada Deposit Insurance Corporation (CDIC) up to a maximum of $60,000. Mutual funds are not covered by deposit insurance.

Derivatives Investments that derive their value from underlying assets such as currencies, treasury bills, and bonds or are linked to indices such as a stock market index. Derivatives can be used to speculate on market movements or to protect investments against major swings in market prices.

Distribution Company A company that has the exclusive right to offer shares of one or more investment funds to the public, directly, or through other investment fund dealers or brokers.

Distribution Fees Assessments levied by some mutual fund companies on the value of units purchased through a back-end load sales option.

Diversification An investment technique intended to minimize risk by placing money in a number of securities. In a diversified portfolio, a decline in the value of one stock, for example, would not dramatically affect the overall value of the holdings.

Dividend Tax Credit A tax credit intended to reduce the effective rate paid on dividend income.

Dividends Payments made to shareholders of a company in the form of cash or additional shares.

Equities Common and preferred shares, representing a share in the ownership of a company.

Equity Mutual Fund An investment fund consisting primarily of common shares, the objective of which is to participate fully in the growth of an economy.

Financial Planners Professionals who specialize in preparing financial programs for individuals, covering such matters as investments, tax planning, retirement preparation, estate planning, and income generation. Some charge an hourly fee while others make their revenue through commissions on the sale of securities, including mutual funds.

Fixed Income Mutual Fund A fund that invests in securities which pay interest at a fixed rate, such as bonds.

Front-End Load The commission charged when mutual fund units are bought.

Global Mutual Fund A fund that invests in several countries, including its home nation. The fund may specialize in stocks, bonds, or money-market instruments.

Growth Fund An investment fund that seeks growth of capital as its primary objective. This type of fund invests primarily in common stocks and securities convertible into common stocks.

Guaranteed Investment Certificates (GICs) Securities issued by financial institutions, such as banks and trust companies, for a specified term. GICs of up to five years issued by members of the CDIC are covered by deposit insurance up to $60,000.

Hedge A strategy used by fund managers to limit investment risk.

Income Fund An investment fund whose primary objective is current income. Such funds generally invest their assets in government, corporate, or other bonds. Some income funds may include high-yielding common stocks.

International Mutual Fund A fund that invests in many countries but not its own.

Investment Objective A fund's (or investor's) goal. Investment strategies can be designed to generate long-term growth, current income, or other goals.

Investment Portfolio Securities owned by an individual consisting of a combination of stocks, bonds, and other types of securities.

Leveraging   Borrowing money for investment purposes.

Liquidity   The ability to convert a security to cash quickly.

Load   The fee charged by a mutual fund to investors to buy units (front-end load or acquisition fee) or sell units (back-end load or redemption fee).

Management Company   The business entity that establishes, promotes, and manages a fund or funds, each of which is a separate entity with its own board of directors or trustee(s).

Management Fee   The fee paid to a fund's manager for investment management and certain administrative services.

Money-Market Mutual Fund   An investment fund, the portfolio of which is invested in large denominations of short-term paper (generally maturing in less than six months), designed to provide high yields with no loss of capital.

Mutual Funds   Pools of investment money, managed by professionals, and invested in a wide range of securities.

Net Asset Value (NAV)   The value of mutual fund shares. It is normally calculated daily by subtracting a fund's liabilities from its assets and dividing by the number of shares outstanding.

No-Load Mutual Fund   A fund offered to the public that carries no purchase fee (front-end load) or redemption fee (back-end load).

Portfolio   The combined holdings of more than one stock, bond, commodity, real-estate investment, cash, or other asset by an individual or institutional investor. The purpose of a portfolio is to reduce risk by diversification.

Principal   The amount of money you invest.

Prospectus   The selling document legally required to be distributed to mutual fund investors. A prospectus describes a fund's investment strategy as well as the risks and costs of the investment.

Redemption   The right of a shareholder to sell, at any time, some or all of his or her shares back to the investment fund for cash.

Registered Investment   Any security that is held in a tax-sheltered plan approved by Revenue Canada.

Registered Retirement Income Fund (RRIF)   A fund set up with proceeds from an RRSP to provide income during retirement.

Registered Retirement Savings Plan (RRSP)   A plan registered with Revenue Canada that encourages Canadians to save for retirement by providing tax relief on contributions and earnings.

Return The amount of money earned by an investment.

Risk The measurable possibility of losing or not gaining value. Risk is differentiated from uncertainty, which is not measurable.

Sales Charge The amount of commission paid by an investor to a sales organization.

Share A unit of ownership in a company.

Shareholder Someone who owns one or more shares in a company.

Stock Ownership in a corporation represented by shares that are a claim on the corporation's earnings and assets. Common stock usually entitles the shareholder to vote in the election of directors and other matters taken up at shareholder meetings or by proxy. Preferred stock generally does not confer voting rights but it has a prior claim on assets and earnings (dividends must be paid on preferred stock before any can be paid on common stock).

Switching Moving money from one mutual fund to another.

Total Return The total amount any investment returns, including any capital gains or losses and any dividends or interest.

Trailer Fee An annual service commission paid by mutual fund companies to sales representatives. These fees generally range between 0.25% and 1% of customers' assets and are paid out of the fund's management expenses.

Transfer Fee The price charged to transfer your assets to another company.

Treasury Bills Short-term debt securities issued most commonly by the federal government.

Unitholder Someone who holds one or more units in a mutual fund.

Volatility The amount by which a fund's return varies over time; used as a measure of investment risk.

Yield Income, usually interest, paid by a security on a regular basis.

Index

third-party funds, 11
top-down management style, 34
Toronto Dominion Bank, 11, 97
Toronto Star, 107
Toronto Stock Exchange (TSE), 77, 101
trailer fees, 10, 17-18, 22

treasury-bill (T-bill) funds, 24, 28, 60
trust companies, 97
TSE Total Return Index (TRI), 29, 72, 101
T3 and T5 slips, 7, 105

volatility, 28, 59, 102
    rating, 29-32, 66, 72

About the Authors

Ranga Chand is one of Canada's leading economists, with a specific interest in and in-depth knowledge of mutual funds. Formerly a senior economist with the investment firm Burns Fry, director of the International Business Research Centre with the Conference Board of Canada, and senior economist with Canada's Department of Finance, his understanding of the fields of domestic and international economics is wide and varied.

Much in demand by organizations, industries, and associations throughout North America, Ranga is well known for his down-to-earth and informative presentations on the subjects of the global economy and investing in mutual funds. He has frequently appeared on CTV's *Canada AM*, CBC *Newsworld*, *Business World*, and other major network TV shows, and has regularly been interviewed by radio and the national print media. He is the author of several books on mutual funds, including most recently his comprehensive, bestselling annual guide, *Ranga Chand's World of Mutual Funds*, published by Stoddart.

Sylvia D. Carmichael is a researcher and writer who has worked with the International Monetary Fund, the British Embassy in Washington, D.C., and Loto Canada in Ottawa. She is now a partner with the Oakville, Ontario, firm Chand Carmichael & Company Limited.

The authors are always interested in hearing from their readers and may be reached by writing to: Ranga Chand, c/o Stoddart Publishing Co. Limited, 34 Lesmill Road, Toronto, Ontario, M3B 2T6.

If you would like information on Chand Carmichael & Company's customized seminars and workshops for corporations and associations, please telephone (905) 844-6708, fax (905) 844-6458, or e-mail chand@idirect.com.